MURDER & CRIME

LEEDS

MURDER & CRIME

LEEDS

Margaret Drinkall

The
History
Press

First published 2012

The History Press
The Mill, Brimscombe Port
Stroud, Gloucestershire, GL5 2QG
www.thehistorypress.co.uk

ISBN 978 0 7524 6637 8

Typesetting and origination by The History Press
Printed in Great Britain

CONTENTS

Acknowledgements

As always, writing a book is a team effort and my grateful thanks go to The History Press and, in particular, Beth Amphlett, who has been encouraging throughout. My grateful thanks go to Leeds Local and Family History Library, where the staff could not have been more helpful and obliging.

I cannot miss the opportunity of mentioning the particular help I received from Eric Ambler of Leeds Town Hall, who gave me a personal guided tour of the courts and the cells where the Leeds Assizes were once held. Knowing that hundreds, if not thousands, of prisoners had stayed there over the years, I asked him if there were ghosts still there and he told of a spooky occasion when he was with a colleague and the heavy, metal doors clanged shut behind them. There was no one near them at the time; the doors are extremely heavy and there is certainly no wind down there. Thank you Eric for that little story!

During the tour, I was able to see the cells beneath the Town Hall, which were very basic, and there certainly would not have been any luxuries for the prisoners – not even bedding. I would also like to thank Mike Roddy, who works at the Town Hall and shared his love of architecture in the city of Leeds, which is a fascinating place to live and work.

Haunted gates?

Introduction

Leeds is an ancient place, which was first mentioned in the Domesday Book. Once the cloth market opened in Briggate in 1684, the burgeoning city began to develop. By the Victorian era, Leeds was a very prosperous place to live. The Industrial Revolution brought an influx of people into the town to work in the factories and workshops and, as a result of this, local businessmen wanted to show off their wealth and affluence, and the city saw massive redevelopment. New buildings such as schools, mechanics institutes and chapels sprang up around the town, paid for by generous benefactors. Leeds officially became a city in 1893, but at the other extreme of all this wealth was severe poverty. Poor housing and overcrowding were common issues

...ggate in Leeds, where the burgeoning city began to develop.

in cities around the country at this time, and Leeds was no exception. Such unsanitary conditions led to an outbreak of cholera in 1849, which killed more than 2,000 people. As in every town and city of this period, there was a criminal underbelly that ran against the grain of those working hard to survive, and drunkenness and domestic violence were rife in the city. It is from this time that the cases explored in this book originate.

Historically, crimes of murder would have first been established at a coroner's court, where the responsibility of the jury was not to prove the guilt of a man or woman but to identify the corpse and establish the cause of death. Many of these felons were then tried at the magistrates' court, from where they would be sent to take their trial at the quarterly Assizes at York. The Assizes for the Yorkshire area were held at York Castle until 6 August 1864,

The old part of Armley Gaol, next to the modern HMP Leeds.

when because of the proliferation of crimes in West Yorkshire they were then held at the Leeds Town Hall. Prisoners who were sentenced to death were usually kept and hanged at Armley Gaol, which was described as a grim, foreboding place, opened in 1847. The gaol is still open as HMP Leeds, which sits next to the modern prison of today. Thankfully, unlike York, there was only one public hanging in front of a crowd of people, before executions were then undertaken inside the gaol. As standard practice, the body would be hung for an hour before being cut down and buried in an unmarked grave within the precincts of the gaol. This was the fate of many of the people who murdered others in Leeds.

The following cases are from the period 1800 to 1900. They are varied and some so complex that even the criminal themselves were incapable of saying why they committed such atrocious acts. Most were committed for gain, whilst others took place through jealousy or after an excess of alcohol. Many of these cases have never been written about before, but all of them happened in and around the city of Leeds all those years ago. Thankfully, little remains of the squalor and overcrowded houses of the past. Beautiful parks abound and today, when I visit Leeds, I find it to be a bustling and rapidly expanding city. What I love most about it is the mix of brand new apartments and commercial buildings alongside older relics of great architectural beauty.

Margaret Drinkall, 2012

Case One

Petit Treason

The Case of Ann Barber, 1821

Suspect:	Ann Barber
Age:	44
Charge:	Murder and Petit Treason
Sentence:	Execution

At the beginning of the nineteenth century, a woman could be charged with the crime of petit treason – the murder of her husband. In law, a man's life was seen as much more valuable than a woman's, and up to the 1790s women convicted of such a crime could be burned at the stake. The murderess in this case was described in one local newspaper as being 'a wretched victim of impure desires'. It is probable that she was convicted as much for her morals as the act of murder itself. So keen were they to convict her, in fact, that she stood charged with the crimes of both murder and petit treason.

Ann Barber was a woman with a past. In 1821, she was forty-four years of age and married to James Barber. She had a child from a previous marriage and two daughters with James Barber, named Hannah, aged 15, and Jane, aged 9. It seems that at this time Ann Barber was cheating on her fifty-year-old second husband with a lodger – a young man from Halifax called William Thompson. At one point, Ann and her lover decided that they were going to elope and they went to live together at Headingley on 21 December. Neighbours reported seeing them leaving the marital home at 6 a.m. with some furniture piled onto a cart. At Headingley, they rented a small cottage, which consisted of one room. They told the landlord, John Holmes, that they were man and wife,

Northgate in Halifax, where William Thompson was from.

but he found out the truth and he threw them out. The couple returned back to Rothwell and, incredibly, her husband allowed the pair of them back into the house. However, the neighbours were not so forgiving and they strongly disapproved of this immoral behaviour. They castigated the couple and James Barber too, calling him a 'cuckold'. Indeed, so much distaste was shown to Thompson that he moved out of the house in February 1821.

Headingley, where the illicit couple went to live.

On Saturday 17 March, Ann Barber roasted an apple for her long-suffering husband, and soon after eating it he became ill. She then warmed him some beer and put sugar in it to soothe him, but he became worse and began to complain of excruciating pain. Despite the fact that there were at least three doctors within a mile of the house, Ann refused to ask one to attend her husband, stating to a neighbour that it would be no use as he would 'surely be dead before morning'. Her prediction came true and her husband died at 3.30 a.m. the following day.

On Sunday, 18 March 1821, Ann was arrested and taken to a public house, where she was held prisoner. She was watched over by the constable's son whose name was George Wadsworth. Without being asked she told him, 'I must tell you the truth about it.' She then confessed to having bought white mercury (arsenic) from a Wakefield druggist, which she had given her husband in two doses – half in the roasted apple and the other half of it in the ale and sugar. She told him that she had done it because she was tired of him. Ann also said that Thompson had offered to marry her 'if anything ailed her husband'. The story of the murder was in the newspapers and the following day an inquest was held on the body. A surgeon, Mr Hindle, examined the corpse and told the coroner that the stomach contents had large amounts of arsenic in it. At the inquest, Ann denied ever having any arsenic, but the coroner was not satisfied and adjourned the inquest to the following Thursday, in order that more

YORKSHIRE ASSIZES.

PETIT TREASON.—*Friday, Aug.* 10.—The trial of ANN BARBER, charged with the wilful murder of her husband, JAMES BARBER, of Rothwell, near Leeds, by administering poison to him, came on this morning, at nine o'clock. We have already reported the particulars of this trial to two o'clock in the afternoon, including the evidence of George Wadsworth, the son of the constable, who swore that the prisoner confessed to him while she was in custody, that she had administered the poison to her husband, because she was tired of him; and it also appeared that she had formed a criminal connexion with another man, of the name of Thompson, with whom she had eloped, but had after-

A newspaper report about the crime of petit treason.

enquiries could be made. The following day she was taken to Wakefield by two constables, the foreman of the jury and the coroner, to visit one of the druggists of that town. In her confession to Wadsworth, she had told him that she had bought a penny worth of white mercury from a druggist called Reinhardt. When the chemist enquired what use it was to be put to, she had told him it was to destroy some mice. The coroner had previously ensured that she was dressed in the same clothes as her previous visit, and she was clearly identified by Mr Reinhardt. Ann Barber categorically denied that she had ever been in his shop, although she reluctantly admitted she might have stood outside the shop. Barber maintained this fiction when the inquest was resumed on Thursday 29 March. The jury quickly found that she was guilty and she was committed to York Castle, for the murder of her husband, at 5 p.m. the same afternoon.

On Friday, 10 August 1821 at 9 a.m., she appeared at the York Assizes in front of the judge, Mr Justice Holroyd. The reporter of the *Leeds Mercury* stated, 'The enormity, and the fortunately rare occurrence of this dreadful crime, excited an unusual degree of interest and the court was crowded, particularly with ladies, at an early hour.' He described the prisoner as being aged about 45 and displaying no particular interest in the case. When she was asked how she pleaded, she responded, 'Not guilty,' in a firm and 'dead sense of voice'. Such was the abhorrence of the crime, the defence requested that no persons from the neighbourhood of Rothwell be appointed on the jury. John Smirthwaite, Ann Barber's brother, spoke about her behaviour with Thompson and how it was reviled in the neighbourhood. Although trying to maintain her indifference, she wept as her little daughter Jane, aged 9, was brought into the courtroom. When Jane saw her mother in the dock, she too covered her face with her hands and cried. Ann became upset and asked if she could have her daughter brought to the bar, but this was not allowed. Her defence stated that he 'would not persist in desiring to examine the child', and the little girl was led out of the court, still crying.

The surgeon, Mr Hindle of Oulton, attended the trial and said that he had examined the deceased man on Sunday 18 March. He later completed the post-mortem and found the coating of the stomach to be very much corroded and with strong signs of inflammation. He stated that symptoms of poisoning would have such an effect, and a sample of the stomach wall confirmed that it was arsenic. The lungs were very black, which also indicated that poisoning had occurred. Mr K.B. Reinhardt, druggist and chemist of Wakefield, said that the prisoner went to his shop between 1 p.m. and 2 p.m. on the afternoon of Friday 16 March. She asked him for a penny worth of white mercury.

Other witnesses spoke of the good health of the deceased man on the days before his death, and neighbours commented on the agony of his last hours. Thomas Spurr told the jury that he had gone into the house at 9 p.m. on the evening of the 16 March, when his friend complained about extreme pain in his bowels. Spurr had suggested to Ann Barber that she call a doctor, but she told him callously that there was no use, as he would be dead before the morning. Her brother-in-law, John Smirthwaite, appeared and told the jury that Barber was very unhappy at being called a 'cuckold', and that it had preyed on his mind. Barber had said that some days 'felt like jumping into a coal pit and ending it all'.

Other witnesses stated that the couple had lived amicably together and that she was a hard worker until Thompson had gone to live with them. The deceased man's mother, Jane Smirthwaite, took the stand and told the court that neighbours would collect around the open door of the house and shout insults to its occupants. Another lodger at the house was a woman called Sarah Parker, who had lived at the house for six years. On the morning of the murder, at 4 a.m., Mrs Smirthwaite had called her from her bed and showed her the body of her son, and Parker helped to lay him out. She described the body as being black with some 'stuff' running out of his mouth.

The judge summed up for the jury and it took them six and a half minutes to find her guilty of petit treason and murder. When asked if she had anything to say as to why the sentence of death should not be carried out, she stated, 'I am sorry that I should be found guilty by false swearing.' The judge put the black cap on his head, but before he could speak she gave a loud shriek and fell to the floor of the dock. It was reported that 'The judge continued with the intonation of the death sentence and grasping the iron bar in front of the dock she looked at him with eyes contorted with terror.' As he continued, she interrupted him time and time again, pleading, apologising and proclaiming her innocence. He said to her:

Ann Barber you have been found guilty of the dreadful crime of murder and a murder of a very aggravated nature inasmuch as it was the murder of your husband whom, by your marriage vows, you were bound to love and cherish. You have been convicted on what has appeared to me the clearest evidence. No reasonable creature can have a doubt of your guilt from the clearness of the proof. Your defence has been conducted very ably and all the objections in points of law which could be made were urged by your counsel. Circumstances show that the poison was administered by yourself and on the very day you bought it. So determined were you on his destruction that you that you said it was not necessary to send for a medical man for he would be dead before morning. This effect you had expected from the deadly poison you gave him.

Urging her to spend what little time she had left in prayer and exhortation to her maker, he then asked if there was any reason why sentence should not be carried out. She appeared bemused by this, until one of the wardresses asked her if she thought that she could be pregnant. She shook her head and then, grabbing the wardress, said to her, 'Oh save me, save me!' Still sobbing, she was removed from the court.

Three days later, on Monday, 13 August 1821, Ann Barber was due to be hung in public at the new drop behind York Castle. It was reported in the *Leeds Mercury* that on the Saturday night, she confessed her crime to one of the wardresses in charge of her as they sat up talking late into the night. She admitted to poisoning her husband twice, but the next day she retracted her statement. Ann also denied it again when asked by the prison chaplain if she had made such a confession. She told him that she was terrified of dying on the scaffold, and asked if there was any way that her sentence could be deferred. The chaplain told her that there was nothing he could do to postpone the day of execution and urged her to make the best use of the time she had left. Four ministers visited her on Sunday to pray with her, but it was noted that she showed little sign of contrition for the actions which had led her to that point. She was also visited by her mother, her youngest daughter and her sister on the day before the execution. Early the next morning, she was taken to a chamber near to the scaffold, where she waited nervously for the appointed hour to arrive. Soon after 10 a.m., the chaplain, Reverend Flower, arrived and he finally received her last confession. She told him that she had also tried to poison her husband a few days before his actual death, but without success.

The sentence of death had included that she be 'drawn to the place of execution'. In order to do this, a kind of hurdle was made from a chair. However, when it was brought into the chamber and attempts were made to sit her in it, there were 'shrieks in a terrible manner for some time' from the convicted woman. In the end, struggling wildly, she was carried the few

Site of the scaffold. (Courtesy of Richard Stansfield)

hundred yards to the scaffold on which she was to die. She continued to be very agitated, and there was no evidence that she either understood or joined in the prayer with the chaplain. Finally, she faced the assembled crowd, but when she saw the noose she cried out piteously, 'Oh God save my soul!' The hangman put the cap over her head and she cried out, 'Oh Lord Jesus, I am a-coming to thee!' The bolt was drawn and after a short struggle she died. So great were her struggles whilst on the scaffold that the *Lancaster Gazette* noted, 'She manifested vigour of motion and strength of nerve that could not be expected from her appearance and manner at her trial.' After an hour, her body was given to the Leeds General Infirmary for dissection. However, it was reported that before the dissection took place, the body was laid out for people to see the following day. It was said that the exhibition attracted a large following, mostly made up of women, eager to see the body of this most notorious murderer.

There is little doubt that Ann Barber was guilty of the crime of murder, and was lucky not to be subjected to the more barbaric fate that other women suffered. The *Leeds Mercury* reported that on Sunday, 29 March 1776, a woman from Scarborough, called Elizabeth Bordington, was burnt at the stake at York for petit treason. She also had been having an illicit affair and was convicted, along with her paramour, for the murder of her husband. Condemnation against women who murdered was partly based on the long-held belief that they should be care givers. But the fate of Ann Barber pales into insignificance when compared to cases of child murder.

SOLVED

A Cure for Teething

The Death of Baby William, 1838

Suspect: Margaret Maynes

Age: 20

Charge: Manslaughter

Sentence: Transportation for life

Having a child out of wedlock during the nineteenth century ensured a miserable existence for both the mother and the child. Blame was always placed on the mother, irrespective of the details of what was seen as her fall from grace. Burdened with a child, many women could not find work and were unable to keep themselves. In this particular case of hardship, the child's grandmother offered to look after her grandson, and it was only when this relationship broke down that the child's life was placed in danger.

Margaret Maynes was aged 20 when she found herself pregnant with an illegitimate child in 1836. When the baby was born, she named it after the father, William Burke, although he had made it clear that he wanted nothing more to do with it. She managed to get a job at a Flax Mill, and the child stayed with her mother, also called Margaret Maynes. The younger Maynes was supposed to pay her mother for keeping the child, but the older woman stated that she had not received any money for the care of the baby. Maynes lodged with a woman called Sarah Wilding of Harpers Yard, Kirkgate, in Leeds, who agreed to let Maynes stay with her, providing that the child lived with the grandmother. Wilding also earned money from telling fortunes, and

A newspaper account of the murder committed by Margaret Maynes of her child, William Burke.

SATURDAY, July 14.

MURDER AT LEEDS.

MARGARET MAYNES (21), was charged with the wilful murder of William Burke, her illegitimate child, at Leeds, on the 12th of April last. Mr. DUNDAS and Mr. OVEREND conducted the case for the prosecution; the prisoner, who was friendless and miserably poor, was defended gratuitously by Mr. BAINES. On the prisoner being placed at the bar, she appeared very much affected, and sobbed aloud. After the case had been stated by Mr. DUNDAS, the following evidence was adduced.

Margaret Maynes, examined by Mr. OVEREND.— I live in Harper's Yard, Kirkgate, Leeds. I formerly kept a lodging-house. The prisoner at the bar is my daughter. I knew the child that died; it was illegitimate. At the time of its death it was sixteen months' old. Previous to her committal the prisoner resided in Crispin-street, Leeds, with a person named Wilding. She was employed in a flax mill; she had not been working for a short time before she was committed. The child lived with me; and sometimes the prisoner gave something for keeping it, and sometimes she did not. She did not give me any fixed sum. On Monday, the 9th of April, I saw the prisoner in my own house. She remained with me until the evening, as both I and the child were unwell. I had given it some nitre on the Sunday, in consequence. It remained with me on the Monday night. A woman

it was said that she had a curious, oval glass through which she persuaded foolish people to look; she would then tell their fortune.

Little William Burke was aged about 16 months at this time and was described by his grandmother as being 'a fine, healthy looking lad'. On Sunday, 8 April 1838, Mrs Maynes had given the child some spirits of nitre, rubbed onto his gums – a compound containing laudanum, which is illegal today. At that time, however, it was used quite widely to quieten fractious children. On the Monday, Mrs Maynes sent for her daughter because both she and the baby were ill. Maynes arrived about at 9 a.m., where she remained until nightfall as the child was teething and poorly. The following day, the child was a little better and Mrs Maynes took him to the house where Maynes lodged on Crispin Street in Leeds. She asked Maynes for a clean apron and when she did get one, she lay the child down on its mother's knee and told her, 'Here is your child; he is poorly. You look after it.' Maynes was not happy, but she took the child and placed him on her knees, trying to pacify him.

On Thursday, Maynes took the baby to her mother's house again and Mrs Maynes noted that William still looked very poorly. When she enquired what was wrong with the baby, Maynes told her that he had taken a fit that morning. She told her mother that she had been to see the local doctor, Dr Ward, that morning, and he had lanced the child's gums because he was teething, but he had seen no evidence of a fit. Dr Ward had given her a bottle of medicine, but she told her mother that she had not given baby William any of it yet. Looking at the child again, Mrs Maynes thought that he looked stupefied and once again asked her if she had given the baby any medicine at all, to which her daughter replied that she had not. Mrs Maynes told her daughter that she did not believe her. Two or three hours afterwards, she saw her daughter again with the baby, who looked to be in the same state as earlier. She demanded that Margaret take the baby to see the doctor again and offered to go with her to see Dr Ward, to which she agreed. Mrs Maynes asked the doctor if he thought that the baby looked sleepy and had possibly been given some laudanum, and she asked Dr Ward to give the child an emetic. The doctor agreed with her and he quickly prepared something which would make the baby vomit. Dr Ward stated that it was his opinion that the child had been fed some laudanum, which Maynes denied once more.

The emetic was given at about 5 p.m., and the prisoner and her child were sent into the kitchen of the surgery to wait for it to take effect. Mrs Maynes returned home for a short while, before returning to the doctor's house. She found her daughter still in the kitchen where she was crying; the child was on her knees. The doctor's wife was also there, and they stayed with the child until midnight, when he expired. Only moments before the child died, Mrs Ward asked her if she had given anything to the child and to tell her the truth. Maynes replied 'Must I?' On being begged 'in the name of God to do so', Maynes then said to Mrs Ward, 'I will tell you the truth.' She said that she had bought a pennyworth of laudanum from a druggist called Mrs Rastrick, which she claimed she had lost, and had been forced to buy some more. She told the doctor's wife, 'I have given William a teaspoonful in some warm tea.' The doctor was told and he informed her that he would have to report the death to the police, to which she replied, 'I do not mind what you do because I never meant to hurt the child.'

Maynes was arrested and taken to the Town Hall where she was locked in a cell. An inquest was held on the body of the dead child in front of the coroner,

Mr John Blackburn Esq. Several witnesses were heard before Maynes told the coroner and the jury that she did give the child the laudanum, but had not intended to kill him. The jury had no option but to find her guilty of wilfully murdering her child, and she was ordered to the next Assizes to take her trial.

Maynes was brought to trial at Leeds on Saturday, 14 July 1838, before the judge, Mr Justice Williams. Sarah Wilding was the first to give evidence. She told how the prisoner had lodged with her whilst the child remained at her mother's. She also said that the prisoner had brought the child to her house on Tuesday 10 April, and she had reminded her that she could not lodge there with a child. She said that whilst she stayed with her, Maynes would often go out on Friday and pawn the cap that the child had on its head, to buy her breakfast. Mrs Wilding had begged her not to do that, to which the prisoner replied, 'Oh he'll never need it,' and went ahead and pawned it.

The next day, she went out to buy some food and came back having had some liquor, but Mrs Wilding told the court that Maynes was not so drunk that she did not know what she was doing. Maynes had said to her that she would kill the baby 'and all of its breed'. Against her landlady's wishes, the child slept with its mother that night and nothing ailed it. In the morning, the prisoner fed the child and, soon after breakfast, Mrs Wilding left the house, leaving the mother and child together. In the course of the afternoon, she saw Maynes in the town centre without the child. Maynes had approached and told her that a friend named Bridget Gorman had come to see her, saying that she had had a dream that baby William was going to die because the prisoner had given it something. She asked her again if she had given William anything and she once more denied it. A juror asked her if she had ever seen Maynes ill-treat the child or whether she had ever witnessed him having a fit. Wilding denied both counts. She also told the court that although they had agreed on a rent of 2s 5d a week, Maynes had not paid a penny for her lodgings.

The magistrates' court at Leeds Town Hall.

City Square in the centre of Leeds.

Next to take the stand was Bridget Gorman – who lodged with the elder Mrs Maynes – who told a different story. She said that the prisoner had often used harsh words to the little boy, although she had never seen her striking him. She said that on one occasion she had said to him 'to be gone out of her sight', as she did not like to see him 'or any of his breed'. She told the court that William had been in a delicate state for about a week before he died. On the Wednesday morning in question, she saw the prisoner standing at the yard end talking to her husband. She joined them and, at the prisoner's request, they went to the Wellington pub and had two-penny worth of rum. When they came out of the pub, the prisoner stopped, saying that she would be back in a minute. She went into a shop at Kirkgate, near to a jeweller's shop. When she came back, she asked them to go into the Royal Oak and there they had some more ale. During the conversation she told the couple that she wanted a small bottle, and her husband said that he had an empty smelling-salts bottle which she could have. The two women then left Mr Gorman in the Royal Oak and both went back to her mother's house.

The child was still in bed but woke up and began to cry. The witness told the court that she had last seen William on Thursday at Mrs Wilding's house, and he was laid on the bed looking very pale and blue around the mouth. The child was asleep and Maynes told her that the child had been ill during the night. Next day, around 4 p.m., she called again and found the baby William was very ill indeed. She had asked Maynes if the child had taken anything to eat and was told that he had eaten some meat.

Mrs Sarah Furniss told the coroner that she was the wife of a druggist in Kirkgate, and on the morning of 11 April, she had sold a pennyworth of laudanum to a woman who came into the shop. She asked her whether she had a container to put the laudanum in and she told her that she hadn't a clean bottle to put it into. The woman said that she would get a bottle and return, which she did later that evening. The woman had told her that she wanted it for another woman who had recently been confined. The druggist's wife asked her if the patient was used to taking laudanum and the woman had replied 'No, only when she had been confined,' and asked her how much she should give her. The druggist's wife told her about ten or twelve drops and she explained to the jury that a pennyworth contained about 120 drops. When asked by the judge if she could identify the prisoner as the woman who had bought the laudanum, she was unable to point out anyone in the room. Mrs Rastrick, also the wife of a druggist of Leeds, said that she had sold the prisoner a penny worth of laudanum as well, at between eleven and twelve o'clock on Thursday 12 April. She had a baby in her arms and she gave the druggist a teacup, which Mrs Rastrick put the laudanum in. The woman told her that she wanted it for her mother who was afflicted with rheumatism. Mrs Rastrick told her that ten drops would be sufficient to relieve her mother of rheumatic pain.

The surgeon, Dr Ward, said that he remembered the prisoner coming to his surgery on 12 April and bringing the baby with her, telling him that her son had a fit. He told the coroner that he had noted that the baby's gums were very swollen and his face was flushed. He had lanced the gums, and throughout this process the child did not cry at all and appeared to be asleep. When asked by a juror, he replied that he could not see any evidence of the child having had a fit. An hour later, the prisoner brought the child back to the surgery again, stating that he had experienced another fit. The surgeon examined the child once more. He noted that the infant's breathing was now quite short and his pupils were contracted. He asked the mother what she had given the child, but the prisoner denied having administered anything. Dr Ward tried to make the child sick by putting a catheter into its stomach, and the baby brought up some wine and water, which was impregnated with laudanum. He kept a sample of the stomach contents in a phial. He then gave the child another emetic, which again brought back regurgitated laudanum. He continued to inject water into the catheter until the stomach contents did not smell of laudanum. The doctor told the jury that no matter how hard he tried to induce the child to vomit again, he was unsuccessful and, despite the injections of some stimulants, the child died at 12.10 a.m.

Later that morning, Mrs Maynes went to the doctor's surgery with a small bottle which had previously held smelling salts. The bottle now held laudanum, which he gave to the constable. During the post-mortem, Dr Ward found no laudanum in the lining of the child's stomach, but he had no doubt that the laudanum administered was the cause of the child's death. He estimated that the amount which had come out of the child's stomach would have been the equivalent of fifty or sixty drops, more than enough to kill a child of that age. Asked by a juror, Dr Ward stated that to give a child more than twenty-five to thirty drops would endanger its life. He also stated that poor people often give their children laudanum as a medicine, although medical men, including himself, know that it is dangerous. He continued, 'It is so common a practice by the humbler classes at the moment, that we tend to make no inquiries and the size of the drops vary by the vessel that they are dropped from.'

The doctor's wife, Mrs Elizabeth Ward, followed her husband onto the stand and her evidence corresponded with his. She said that at the time the prisoner was in the kitchen, her mother asked her repeatedly whether she had given the baby something, which she always denied. As the child became increasingly ill, Maynes told Mrs Ward that she had bought some laudanum, lost it, and then bought some more from a woman in a shop on Marsh Lane. She also told her that her landlady had complained about the child keeping her awake at night, and that she had been compelled to give it something to make it quiet. Mrs Ward told the court that she had not heard the woman say anything bad to the child and appeared to be quite distressed when the he died.

The prisoner's defence, Mr Baines, addressed the jury and told them that he had been appointed at the last minute as the prisoner was 'friendless and miserably poor'. He said that he had 'taken on the task gratuitously', and continued, 'If I had not confidence in the jury I would be overwhelmed with the weight of responsibility of the case.' He told them that he did not intend calling any witnesses, as Maynes had been very open about the fact that she had bought the laudanum and had administered it to the child in his illness. He also told them that Sarah Wilding's evidence was not to be trusted as she made her living by telling fortunes. The jury had to make up their minds as to whether the prisoner had administered the laudanum to help take away the child's teething pain, or in order to end its life. He said that there was not a shred of evidence that the prisoner had acted by any unworthy motive. Indeed, he told them, Maynes had been exceedingly distressed when the child had died. The comments that she made towards it when she was intoxicated were to be dismissed. But if they found she had acted carelessly or negligently, they would have to find a verdict of manslaughter. He said that if they had any doubt about her guilt, then the verdict should be given in her favour.

The judge summed up the case minutely and said to the jury that the question they had to consider was whether the prisoner had administered the laudanum with intent to destroy life, or if it had been given to relieve the child from pain and, in ignorance and carelessness, had lead to fatal results. It took the jury only thirty minutes to find her guilty of manslaughter. The case had occupied the court for six hours and she was then told to stand down.

Three days later, Margaret Maynes was brought back into the court for sentencing. The judge, Mr Justice Williams, told her that although she had been indicted for murder, the jury had found her guilty of manslaughter and that he was not at all satisfied with the verdict. He declared:

The stairs that lead up into court, where Margaret Maynes would have heard her sentence.

The jury asked for a recommendation to mercy and normally I would be most anxious, careful and scrupulous to attend to such a recommendation. But after a careful perusal of my notes and deep consideration, I found the case so strong against you that I could not consider, with my utmost responsibility, to do otherwise than pass the sentence I am about to do. It is always to me a most unwelcome duty and particularly so when I have to neglect a jury's recommendation without severe punishment.

He then sentenced her to be transported beyond the seas for the rest of her natural life. Maynes was one of 143 convicts transported on the *Mary Ann*, which left these shores on 16 July 1839 – bound for the colony of New South Wales – to begin her life sentence.

Despite the judge's decision, the case does seem to have some mitigating circumstances. The mother was very young and, at the age of 21, she was not perhaps as careful as she should have been in the administration of what was generally accepted as medicine. Laudanum was widely used by parents, both married and unmarried, as a soporific agent to be used during teething; therefore it cannot be viewed as the poison we regard it today. However, what the case skates over is that the child was living with the grandmother, and only when she took the little boy and gave it back to its mother, stating 'You look after it,' did the problems begin. Having employment, and so not able to look after her child, Maynes was placed in a very difficult situation. Her landlady had categorically stated that she would not have the child in her house, so what was she to do? Whether or not the laudanum was administered lawfully or with intent to kill, we shall never fully know, but regardless, Maynes had the rest of her life to regret her actions of that night.

Case Three

Murder in Bell and Bull Yard

A Case of Domestic Violence, 1838

Suspect:	Joseph Gilpin
Age:	40
Charge:	Murder
Sentence:	Ten Years' Transportation

The following case of domestic violence caused much distress, due to the fact that the poor woman was heavily pregnant when she was murdered. In those days, it was impossible to get a divorce and the only solution was to live separately. The victim in this case lived in a different residence from her husband – which was all she could do to get away from his violence. Comments made by the judge reveal a more tolerant attitude towards domestic violence than would be accepted today, but despite this, he gave the highest sentence he was able to, within the boundaries of the law, to ensure that the man would be an example to other violent husbands.

The Bull and Bell Yard, Briggate, Leeds, was a typical court of the Victorian era. Every neighbour knew everyone else in the yard, although one newcomer had tried to keep herself to herself. On the evening of 23 October 1838, a resident in the court was Ann Greenwood, who lived with her mother and sister, Mary. Her mother, Jesse Ward, went to answer the door when someone knocked a little after 8.15 p.m. The man at the door was about 40 years of age, and asked her mother if she knew where his wife, Elizabeth Gilpin, lived. Mrs Ward directed him to the house next-door-but-one to her own. Ann looked out the window and she saw the man knock on the door and enter the house. Within three minutes, Ann and her mother heard a 'scuffling' sound and their neighbour, Mrs Gilpin, scream out. As both mother and daughter rushed outside, they saw Mrs Gilpin on her hands and knees outside her own door. She was heavy with child but that didn't stop the man from kicking her in the face. As he went to kick her again, Mrs Ward bravely rushed up to him and pushed him away from his wife. She told him, 'Get away from her,' and stood in between the man and the injured woman. As he went out of the yard, Mrs Ward called after him that he was a 'murdering thief'. He turned round and told her, 'if I have not done it, if I have not murdered her, I will come back and do it. I will be Mrs Gilpin's butcher and yours likewise.' Without further ado he left the yard, and Mrs Ward and Ann Greenwood immediately rushed to help the injured woman.

Mrs Gilpin was so badly hurt that she could not stand up. She crawled on her hands and knees to the door of Mrs Ward's house. Her cap had been torn off her head and she had two wounds, one over each eye where she had been kicked. Blood was pouring down her face and she was crying. Mrs Gilpin told Ann and her mother, 'Lord have mercy on my soul, for I am a murdered woman and I shall never get better again.' Gently she was lifted to her feet and lay on the sofa at Mrs Ward's house, whilst Ann ran to fetch a doctor. A surgeon who lived nearby, Mr Nelson, attended to her injuries and gave her something to sooth the pain. Later that night, Mrs Ward escorted the dying woman back to her own house at 10.30 p.m. Ann, who could see that the poor woman was in a bad state, elected to remain in the house with her. Mrs Gilpin had a daughter and two sons who lived with her, but none of them were in when the incident happened. On Sunday 28 October, the poor woman died of her injuries.

The police had been called in and had taken statements from Ann, her sister and mother, and from Mrs Gilpin. As a result of this, Gilpin was apprehended later on the night of the attack. He was seen in Vandyke Street, which was about half a mile's distance from Bull and Bell Yard. The night constable George Hall, who knew him, approached and said, 'Joseph I have come for you.' Gilpin replied, 'Yes I expected that someone would come for me and I didn't go to bed.' He told Hall the reason why he had attacked his wife. It seems that the couple had separated a few months before, despite the fact that she was pregnant with his child.

Gilpin said that his wife had sent him a note a week earlier, asking for £10 to get one of their sons apprenticed. He showed Hall the note and he read it, before asking Gilpin to come to the courthouse, where he was taken into the charge room and arrested by the Chief Superintendent, Mr William James. When asked why he had attacked his wife in such a ferocious a manner, Gilpin told him that this was not the first time his wife had asked for money. He made a statement saying that earlier in the summer she had written him a note asking for money to get both lads apprenticed, and she had promised that if he gave her £30 she would not bother him again. The latest note asked him to take the two boys to live with him, as she was having problems managing one of them, James. Gilpin had gone to the house but she told him that if he didn't give her the money to get James apprenticed, then she would get him taken into prison for failing to maintain his children. The prisoner stated that he had then got angry and hit her and kicked her, but he never thought it would be her death stroke. He blamed it on the fact that he had been drinking for the past three days, but confessed that he had intended 'going to her house to give her a right walloping'. Gilpin told the arresting officer that while he was there, he intended to 'do the job right' because he didn't want to be sent to the Wakefield House of Correction again. It became apparent that he had served sentences for violence to his wife twice before.

A typical night constable.

Gilpin was charged with the attempted murder of his wife and, the next day, was brought into the magistrates' court. When the Chief Superintendent, who had arrested Gilpin, heard five days later that his wife had died, he re-arrested Gilpin for murder. The magistrate asked if the man had been intoxicated when he was found. The Chief Superintendent replied that he thought that Gilpin might have been slightly intoxicated, but not so much that he did not know what he was doing.

Evidence was given by Mrs Ward, Ann Greenwood and the surgeon. The jury took just half an hour to return a verdict of guilty of manslaughter, and sent him to take him trial at the next Assizes. The inquest on Mrs Gilpin was heard on Wednesday, 7 November 1838, when once more the evidence was given by Mr Nelson, the surgeon, Jessie Ward and her daughter, Ann. Ann told the court that she had visited her neighbour a few times after the attack, but she didn't like to go in as her face made her feel ill. Mr Nelson gave an account of the several conversations he had held with the woman before she died. He told the court that she had received a severe beating at Gilpin's hands five months previously, and that was the reason she left him. He gave his opinion that death was caused by the injuries inflicted on her by Gilpin on the night of 24 October 1839.

The coroner then adjourned the inquest until the following Wednesday, in order that further enquiries could be made. At the resumed inquest – before Mr Hopps, the deputy coroner for Leeds – Gilpin was present. John Hall, the brother-in-law to Gilpin, gave evidence that he had seen Mrs Gilpin sat in an armchair in Mrs Ward's house after her husband had attacked her. She was bleeding profusely from the wound on her head. He asked her what had happened and she told him that her son James had been 'rude' to her, so she had applied at the workhouse to have him put out as an apprentice. They told her that her husband must do it and this was the reason that she had sent him the note. Hall said that he helped the poor woman to her bed, where she repeated that she was a 'murdered woman'. The night watchman, George Hall, gave evidence about the night that he had arrested Gilpin. The jury took only five minutes to return a verdict of guilty of wilful murder, and the magistrate sent him to take his trial at the next Assizes.

Gilpin appeared at the Assizes on 9 March 1839, in front of the judge, Mr Baron Alderson. Mr Baines and Mr Hill were for the prosecution and Sir Gregory Lewin defended the prisoner. The first person to give evidence was Ann Greenwood. She told the court about the attack on the pregnant woman and how her mother had bravely gone to stop the attack. She said that Gilpin had used much violent language, both to herself and her mother, and had threatened to come back and finish them off. Her sister, Mary, and her mother corroborated the evidence. Mr Garlick, a surgeon of Leeds, told the jury that on Tuesday 30 October, he had conducted a post-mortem with Mr Nelson. He had found that the deceased had wounds over each eye and swelling on the right side of the face, extending down the neck as far as the breast. Mr Garlick told the jury that whilst examining the cavity of the head, he had found that the brain was much congested with blood. He said, 'External violence has been applied with the greatest severity on the face and the right side of the jaw.' One of the jury asked what Mr Garlick thought would cause such injuries; he told him that a violent kick by a strong boot would produce such injuries. The judge asked him to give his opinion on how long the injuries could have been inflicted and he told him that it had been done within the week. Mr Garlick concluded that, in his opinion, death was caused due to the extreme violence suffered by Mrs Gilpin. Mr James, the Chief Superintendent, told the judge that when Gilpin was brought in to the police station, he had confessed to giving her 'a damned good walloping', and added that he had 'not half done it'.

The judge summed up the evidence for the jury, telling them that they had to distinguish whether this was a case of murder or manslaughter. He asked them 'Did this man go to his wife's house with the intention of killing her?' He told them that if he had just intended to give her a severe beating, and as a result of that she had died, then they would have to find him guilt of manslaughter. He almost seems to have been defending the prisoner when he said:

> In the first place the prisoner did not use a weapon. He certainly used great brutality, but it does not necessarily follow that he intended to kill her, but only that he intended to give pain. His behaviour was very wicked and improper, but perhaps the crime only amounts to aggravated manslaughter. He acted upon impulse and gave her two or three unlucky blows, which ended in her death.

The jury took little time to find Gilpin guilty of manslaughter. In a seeming reversal of attitude, the judge then made his abhorrence of domestic violence clear when he addressed the prisoner. He told him that it was a most aggravated case and said, 'You went to see your wife, who was far gone with child, and in an inhumane and brutal manner caused her death.' He pointed out that Gilpin had shown no remorse whilst confessing his crime to the two police officers, and he had also shown great violence to the women who had tried to defend his wife from him. His Lordship stated that the prisoner was a strong, athletic man and that his wife, because of her condition, could not have withstood his assault. The prisoner, at this point, said to the court that he did not intend to kill her. The judge ignored him and stated that, in order to deter other men from committing the same offence against their wives, the offender would be transported for ten years.

A prison hulk, like the one that Joseph Gilpin boarded in 1839.

The *Leeds Mercury* reported that Gilpin was a man of dissolute habits and, by his own admission, had reduced himself to a more or less permanent state of intoxication – almost to a state of madness. This insanity had been demonstrated a few months previously, when had been so desperate for money for drink that he had sold a legacy of £80, which was payable in a few months, for the sum of £40. On 6 May 1839, it was reported that Joseph Gilpin had been sent from York Castle to the *Justitia* hulk at Woolwich, to await transportation. Records show that Gilpin was transported on the convict ship *Layton*, on 9 July 1839, to begin his ten-year sentence in Van Diemen's Land, which is now Tasmania.

Drink was a key factor in this case. Many philanthropists in Leeds tried, without success, to curb licensing laws and to introduce the Temperance Movement to the people. But the reality of it was that working-class men and women enjoyed the social life in the many pubs and beer houses of the city, and needed an escape from the rat-infested slums in which they were forced to live.

Case Four

Was it the Salt Man?

The Mystery of Christopher Winder's Death, 1841

Suspect: Thomas Millett

Charge: Wilful Murder

Sentence: Acquitted

The next case is an unsolved one, where the judge took the decision to stop proceedings as there was just not enough evidence to convict the prisoner, Thomas Millett. Nevertheless, a man had been killed on the highway, under some very curious circumstances indeed, and the convicted man acted very suspiciously. Both men were intoxicated and Millett appeared to have been so drunk that he lost his horse and cart. Had the prisoner, Millett, got away with murder?

There was some consternation on Friday, 6 June 1841, when the body of Christopher Winder, aged 53, was found on the turnpike road between Leeds and Stanningley, at almost 11.30 p.m. The body was found by two men named Robert Grayshon and Joseph Gaunt, who had been travelling down the road in a cart, when Gaunt said to his companion that there was a body behind them in the road. The road was under repair and, as a consequence, there were piles of stones of all shapes and sizes all over the surface. They stopped the cart and had a closer look. They discovered several marks of violence on the man, who was laid on his back. Around his head and shoulders were a number of large stones, some of which had blood and hair on them. The man lay in a large pool of blood and had severe bruising all over his face.

PC Goodson from Bramley was called and went to the scene immediately. He asked the two men if the cart could have possibly gone over the body, but the two men denied having felt anything at all until Gaunt looked behind him and saw the body. PC Goodson then helped the two men take the body to the Barley Mow Inn, at Bramley. Winder had earlier been seen at a public house, the Rose and Crown, run by his nephew, Samuel, who made a statement that his uncle was wearing a blue smock and a blue cap when he came into the pub for a drink. By trade Christopher Winder was a slubber, but he had been out of work for more than two years. He went to the Rose and Crown around 2 p.m. and stayed until about 7 p.m. When he left, he carried a bundle which contained two silk handkerchiefs and some bread.

In the pub at the same time was a 30-year-old man called Thomas Millett, an Irishman who came from Halifax, but was well known in the area as an itinerant dealer in salt. It was reported that he had been in the pub from 5 p.m. until 10 p.m. and he had put his horse and cart into a nearby shed. Samuel Winder told the police that both men had been in the tap room and there had been no quarrel that he was aware of, but that both men were a bit 'worse for wear', although he judged that they were able to walk properly. There was a lot of distrust against Irish people at that time, so when Millett was leaving the landlord told two men to 'make sure that he got out of town safely'. The two men returned after about a quarter of an hour to say that he had gone on his way. Millett was next seen by William Binns, a toll keeper employed at the Cocksbutt Lane toll bar. He asked Binns if he wanted to buy any salt, but the offer was turned down and Millett became abusive – nevertheless, he paid the toll fare of 4½d. Binns watched him walking behind his horse and cart, and noted that he seemed to be quite drunk. The toll keeper then retired to bed and the only interruption to his sleep was a man on another horse and cart, which passed through the toll bar around 1 a.m.

Landlord Francis Scott kept the Fleece Inn and had served Christopher Winder at around 9 p.m. the same night. Winder had left the pub at approximately 10 p.m. and Scott saw him walking towards Armley. He later told the police that he did not hear any quarrelling or noise for the remainder of that night. The first thing he knew about the murder was when he was told that a man's body had been found further down the road. Meanwhile, Samuel Winder had closed up the Rose and Crown and was in the bar area with his wife and her elderly father, around midnight. So he was surprised when someone started kicking at

SHOCKING MURDER NEAR BRAMLEY.

Within the last few days the inhabitants of Bramley and surrounding neighbourhood have been thrown into a state of considerable excitement by the discovery of a murder committed under circumstances of great atrocity, on the Leeds and Blenningley road, and within about 900 yards of Cockshott-lane bar. We had prepared a detailed account of the proceedings at the inquest, held before John Blackburn, Esq., at the Barley Mow Inn, Bramley, on Monday and Tuesday last, but an overwhelming pressure of electioneering and other matter renders us unable to do more than give the mere facts of the case The name of the deceased was Christopher Winder, aged 63, a slubber, residing at Bramley, and that of the man who is supposed to be implicated in his death, Thomas Millett, an Irishman, and a salt hawker, living at Bradford. The circumstances tending to point him

A newspaper report documenting the finding of Christopher Winder's body.

the pub door. He went to the locked door and shouted out to ask who it was, and Millett replied, 'It's the salt man damn you.' Winder opened the door and Millett demanded a bed for the night. The landlord told him that there were no beds available and advised him to return back to his horse and cart as he shut the door. Millett then craftily went round the back of the pub and entered by a back door which had been left open. Once again, he demanded a night's lodging, stating that he could pay. He threw down a sixpenny piece, but offered to pay up to 2s. He did not say anything to the landlord and his wife about being robbed. Samuel Winder told him that he had to go and, showing little sympathy, threw him out after about ten more minutes.

An inquest was held on Monday, 7 June 1841 at the Barley Mow Inn, before the coroner, John Blackburn Esq. Samuel Winder told the inquest that when Millett returned back to the Inn to demand a bed, he was wearing the blue cap which had been worn by the deceased earlier that evening. The cap, which was produced in court, was made of blue serge material and it was examined by the jury. PC Joseph Goodson told the coroner that he had been awakened on the night of the murder by two men who had knocked at his door at around 11.45 p.m. The men told him that there was a horse and cart in front of his house. He examined the cart to find a quantity of salt and some weights and scales in the back. It was whilst he was putting the horse and cart into a shed that Gaunt and Grayshon arrived, telling him that they had found a body in the road. He told the coroner that he had brought several of the stones

The town of Halifax, seen here from Beacon Hill.

from around the body and produced them at the inquest. The stones weighed between 1½lbs and 11½lbs, and many had blood and hair sticking to them. Goodson said that he had returned back to the scene of the crime later that night, around 3 a.m., and found a blue cap, a small key and a pencil near to where the body had been found. Searching further, he found a bundle with some bread in it and two handkerchiefs.

Goodson then returned back to the Barley Mow public house, where he had examined the body, and found the waistcoat pocket on the right side had been turned inside out. He also noted that clothes on the body were covered in dust, as if the deceased man had put up a struggle. The key on the body was later found to fit a locked box the dead man had kept at his sister's house. When Samuel Winder had been shown the bundle, he identified them as belonging to his uncle. In answer to a question from one of the jury, Goodson said that both Grayshon and Gaunt were sober on the night they found the body.

The next to give evidence was George Aveyard, the toll keeper at Stanningley, who told the coroner that the man known as Millett had appeared at his toll gate at 3 a.m. on the Saturday morning, looking for his horse and cart. He told him that he had been travelling down the road when he had been attacked by an unknown man; he showed the toll keeper the scratches and bruises which had been made on his arm by his assailant. The toll keeper formed the impression of a man that had been out all night and who had been involved in a fight. Millett told them that his attacker had taken about 25s, leaving him with just 6d. He told Aveyard that he had gone into a pub that evening for something to eat and had set off at dusk. Then he had seen the man who robbed him of his horse and cart. Aveyard asked him if he was drunk and he agreed that he was rather 'fresh'.

Another toll-bar keeper, from the Calverley Moor turnpike road, spoke about Millet looking for his horse and cart around 4.30 a.m. on the Saturday morning. He asked the toll keeper to hold onto the horse and cart for him if he found it. He also commented that Millett's clothes appeared to be covered in dust, as if he had rolled in the road. Another witness, Richard Robinson, spoke about himself and a friend passing the Leeds to Stanningley road on the Friday night at around 10.30 p.m., and seeing two men in the road. One was lying on his back whilst the other was kneeling over him. The man kneeling said to the passing men, 'Gentlemen, will you help me to make this man be quiet.' Robinson ignored the comment and proceeded past him, and then heard a sound which could have been a blow or a body falling. He told the coroner that he did not know either of the men.

William James, the Chief Superintendent, took his place and told the coroner that after hearing from all the witnesses, he had gone to Bradford and arrested Thomas Millett. He also took two constables – James Winder and Daniel Roberts – with him. Millett was charged with the murder of Christopher Winder, the night before at Bramley, and Millett replied that he knew nothing about it. Mr James then took him to the White Bear pub, where his clothes were examined and he was found to have bloodstains on the right knee of his trousers. Millett maintained that the blood on his trousers had come from a cut knee sustained in the struggle with the man on the night of the murder. Bloodstains were also found on his waistcoat and his shirt, and the wristband of his shirt on the left arm had been torn off. Later, when Millett was locked in the police cells, Mr James examined the trousers more carefully and found the blood was only on the outside of the knee. Millett again repeated his story that he had met a man on the road who had robbed him of his money. He claimed that the man had beaten him so savagely that he had been forced to retaliate, feeling that it was a case of 'kill or be killed'.

PC Winder asked him why there were so many stones near the dead man's head, and Millett told him that he had thrown them at his attacker once he went down onto the road. Millett also told Mr James that once he had got the man down on the floor, he had run back to the public house where he wanted to stay for the night, but the landlord wouldn't let him have a bed. Millett said he had then gone into a shed, where he stayed for the night, and the next morning had sent his wife to find the missing horse and cart.

After taking his statement, Mr James then took Millett to the stable of the Barley Mow and showed him Winder's body. He asked him if that was the man who had attacked him and he identified him positively. He also identified the blue cap which had been found at the side of the body as being his.

The medical evidence caused great astonishment to the coroner when the surgeon, Mr T.P Teale, gave evidence that he had examined the body of Christopher Winder on the morning of Saturday 6 June. He noted that the deceased had a large wound on his chin and that his head and hands were bloody. When he opened up the body for a post-mortem, he had found contusions on the upper part of his shoulders and thighs. The head and scalp had taken a terrific beating, but Mr Teale offered the view that he did not think they had been inflicted by falling down onto the stones. In his opinion, the death had been caused by the fractured skull and the accompanying injury to the brain. The surgeon stated that in his estimation, the injuries were more consistent with a cart wheel going over the head. Having examined the road where the body had been found, Mr Teale suggested that the road was not wide enough for a cart to pass around the body, and the injuries were consistent with one wheel going over the head, and another wheel causing the injuries to the lower part of the body.

The prisoner was then asked if he had anything to say, and he stated simply that after being robbed, he had returned back to the Rose and Crown. Millett claimed to have told the landlord that he had been robbed when he had asked for a bed for the night. As was customary, all the evidence during the inquest was written down, but when Millett was given it to sign, he hesitated and said that he didn't know what they were talking about. He spoke to one of the policemen who stood near to him to ask if he could have the statement read out again. This was done, and when it was handed to him a second time, he hesitated once more. Turning to the coroner he said, 'What do you say, I have been killing this man?' The coroner replied that he had said no such thing. The prisoner, after hesitating, put a cross on the document and said that was all the statement he wanted to make. As it was 9.30 p.m. by this time, the coroner adjourned the inquest to the following evening at 5 p.m. The prisoner was then transported back to Leeds under a strong entourage of policemen.

There was a great crowd of people outside the Barley Mow Inn when the inquest was resumed the next day. They were all anxious to see the prisoner

The gates leading into the Bridewell.

as he was brought back from Leeds police station, where he had spent the night. The coroner summed up for the jury, stating that he did not agree with the surgeon on all the points he had made. He told them that if a person attacks another to such an extent that he is left insensible in the road and unable to move, in the event of a cart wheel going over him, the attacker was still guilty of murder. He used an example of a man hitting another man with his fist, telling them, 'You wouldn't say the intention was murder in this case, but if he hit a man with a large stone or a piece of wood or iron, the intent would be clear'. He went on to say that Millett had been seen, clearly wearing the hat of the deceased, and his own cap had been found near the body, implicating him very deeply in the crime. It took the jury two hours before they returned with a verdict of guilty of wilful murder, and the prisoner was ordered to York Castle to take his trial. When Millett left the Barley Mow Inn, it was reported that a large group of people had assembled before it to see him leave. As Millet appeared, he was booed and hissed at before being bundled into the police coach.

On Saturday, 17 July 1841, Millett was brought to the Assizes at York before the judge, Mr Justice Wightman. The judge heard all of the evidence and, once again, the surgeon Mr Teale took the stand and repeated his evidence. To the jury's amazement, the judge then stopped the case and, turning to the jury, instructed them to find Millett not guilty. Millett, looking much relieved, left the dock.

Had Millett committed the murder? He certainly acted rashly and suspiciously. The evidence of the surgeon meant that the judge believed that Winder had been killed by a cart wheel going over the body, but could that have been done by Grayshon and Gaunt who had found the body? They only saw it from behind, although it is doubtful that they would have felt it if the wheel had, indeed, gone over the body of a man lying in the road. It is something that, from this distance in time, we will never know.

UNSOLVED

An Evil Ménage à Trois

The Curious Poisoning of Sarah Scholes, 1842

Suspects: Joseph Scholes and Margaret Dowie

Charge: Poisoning

Verdict: Insufficient Evidence

This case was judged not so much on justice, but on the morality of the people concerned. At one point, while revelations were being made, the coroner openly showed his disgust and wanted to bring the hearing to a close. In the end, the verdict was inconclusive but this is still a good example of how morals were judged in the nineteenth century.

Sarah Scholes was a woman possessed. Her husband was Joseph Scholes, who had worked for the Leeds Water Works company. There had been several incidents of domestic violence and stories about his immorality and, as a consequence, he had been 'released' from his occupation. Fortunately, he had managed to get other employment at Kirkstall Grange, near to Kirkstall Abbey, the house of William Beckett MP. The main cause for Sarah's unhappiness was when her husband brought another woman, a prostitute named Margaret Dowie, to live with them at their house on Meadow Lane, Leeds. At that time there was only one marital bed, so Mrs Scholes was thrown out and she was forced to sleep at a neighbour's house. Two years later – probably the worst humiliation for her – he was sleeping in the small, box bedroom and she was forced to share a bed with Dowie.

On 14 December 1842, the dead body of Sarah Scholes was found at the house and it was thought that she had been poisoned by her husband and his paramour. An inquiry was held at the Leeds Courthouse, in front of coroner John Blackburn Esq. and a respectable jury.

The first to give evidence was a neighbour called Moses Long, who explained to the jury that he was the manager of Smith's Mill and had known Mrs Scholes for some weeks. He said that at almost midnight on Tuesday 13 December, he was called to come to the house, where Dowie told him that Sarah had drank some poison out of a brown bottle. In an upstairs bedroom he saw Mrs Scholes, who was laid out on the bed. She did not speak, although her mouth was moving, and she appeared to be insensible. Dowie, who was also in the room, appeared to be much agitated and alarmed. A surgeon, Mr Robert Craven, was sent for but shortly after he arrived, Mrs Scholes died. The surgeon at the inquest told the coroner that he had been called in to see the deceased woman at 12.15 a.m. Her husband had come to his house and told him that his wife had taken poison. When he asked Scholes how he knew, he stated that she had drunk it out of a bottle in front of him and then thrown the bottle down, telling him that she had just taken some prussic acid. When asked why she had done it, he told the surgeon that it was down to jealousy.

Craven told the jury that when he arrived at the house, he found Mrs Scholes lying on the bed, fully clothed, and it was obvious that she was very close to death. Her clothing showed no sign of being disarrayed; her eyes were very bright and not moving, and, from the smell of her breath, he could tell that she had taken prussic acid. He examined the bottle and found it was a phial, which would contain about an ounce of liquid. He tasted what was left and agreed that it was indeed prussic acid. Craven told Scholes that he would show him where the night watchmen would be on his rounds, in order to alert the police to the death of his wife. The surgeon told the coroner that since the death, he had performed a post-mortem and made tests on the stomach and its contents. He had no doubt that the ingestion of prussic acid was the cause of her death.

The wife of Moses Long, Jane, was next to give evidence. She told the court how she had known Mr and Mrs Scholes and Dowie for a few weeks prior to the death. Although she had been in the dead woman's house on many occasions when her husband and Dowie had been present, she had not witnessed any quarrelling between them. They all seemed to live amicably in this strange ménage à trois. On the night of the death, she looked at Scholes and asked him what he had done. He replied that he had done nothing and that Sarah had done it to herself. Apparently, she had refused to accompany Dowie

Kirkstall Abbey.

to bed and had quarrelled with her husband before going into the little box room. Sarah refused to sleep, saying she would sit up all night. Dowie had taken a candle and gone to bed, but woke up a while later and realised that Sarah was still in the other room. Dowie then got up, threatening that she would make Sarah come to bed.

It was then, according to Mrs Long's summary, that Dowie noticed something about Sarah's posture that made her suspicious, and demanded to know what she had in her pockets. Mrs Scholes told her to 'never mind her pockets' as she had 'nothing in them to do with her'. Meanwhile, hearing the commotion, Scholes woke up and said that they would all stay up all night, but as he rose from the bed, Sarah dashed out of the room. Almost immediately she came back into the bedroom and, producing a small bottle, she drank the contents, stating, 'I am poisoned. May the Lord receive my poor soul.' Dowie then told Sarah that she would not let her sleep with her husband.

Leeds Town Hall, where the inquiry into the death of Sarah Scholes took place.

PC Thomas Spiers gave evidence next. He described being called to the house at about 12.30 a.m., where he viewed the body of the dead woman. He asked for the pockets of the deceased to be searched, but all she had in them was a key. Scholes told the constable that one of the keys was to a workbox, which his wife had kept in the sitting room. Spiers opened the box and found two packets labelled 'poison'. These, he told the jury, contained prussic acid. He was asked about the behaviour of Scholes and Dowie, and stated that Scholes appeared calm, but Dowie seemed to be 'fretting'.

Silence fell over the court when Margaret Dowie took the stand. She began by telling the coroner she had known Scholes for over two years. He had 'kept her' before that in a house on Union Street, which had been described as 'a house of ill-fame'. He presented himself as unmarried, but before long he admitted that he had a wife. He told her that he had confessed to his wife about the affair and, to her surprise, Mrs Scholes appeared at her door on Union Street, requesting that she come and live with them both. She told Dowie that her husband was ill and promised that the couple would find her a situation and look after her. She went for a short while, but then left and went to live with a couple named Cookson, who had a house near Roundhay Park, where she learned dressmaking and posed as their niece. However, she was taken ill and Scholes went to fetch her one day and took her into lodgings. But only a few weeks later, he once again took her to live at home with him and his wife. Once more, she left and spent four months in Scotland, before receiving a letter from him asking her to return back to Leeds, saying that he and his wife had separated on her account. However, when he was not in the house, Mrs Scholes would turn up on the doorstep. Dowie asked her to come back, saying, 'Let us all live comfortably together again.'

Mrs Scholes did return to live at the house, but, shortly afterwards, Dowie left to go to live with Scholes at Halifax, where he was working. At this point, the coroner exploded with rage, stating, 'Really gentlemen, this is a most disgraceful statement; I have scarcely patience to listen to it.' Nevertheless, Dowie was asked to continue with her statement. She told the jury that she had returned to Leeds and had gone to live at a lodging house owned by a woman named Robinson, where Scholes continued to visit her.

Again, Scholes claimed that he and his wife had separated and that he had agreed to pay her maintenance each week. Dowie also told the jury that she knew Scholes had not slept with his wife in the last two months, as he had slept in a 'turn-down bed in a room where his tools [were]'. The coroner interjected: 'Well, I think the jury perfectly understand the terms on which this man, his wife and you have been living for the last two or three years, and a more disgraceful exhibition I have never heard. You will now tell us as to the proceedings on Tuesday night.'

Dowie reported that on Tuesday morning, the three of them had taken breakfast together before Scholes went out at around 10 a.m. She and Mrs Scholes had also gone out together but separated, in which time Dowie went to find a milliner's shop at Hunslet. She then met up with a friend and did not see Mrs

Roundhay Park, where Margaret Dowie learned dressmaking.

Scholes again until she got home later that night at approximately 7.30 p.m. She stayed at home with Mrs Scholes while the husband went out again; she claimed that there was no quarrel between any of them. Scholes returned home and went to sleep in the box bedroom, where Dowie and Mrs Scholes went to find him. According to Dowie, she could see that Mrs Scholes was not ready to go to bed so, taking the candle, she left the pair together. She fell asleep but at some point woke up and realised that Mrs Scholes had still not come to their shared bed. She went into the box room, where she found Mrs Scholes still sitting in the room as she had left her. Dowie asked twice, 'Why don't you come to bed tonight like other nights.'

When questioned by the coroner, Dowie told him that she had not threatened Mrs Scholes to make her go to bed. Mr Scholes had woken up and told his wife to go to bed, but she replied that she wouldn't go for either of them. Scholes had made a motion to rise out of his bed and his wife ran out of the room.

It was then that Mrs Scholes took the poison, after which Dowie ran for help from the neighbours whilst Mr Scholes removed his wife into the double bed. When Dowie returned, she found him holding his wife and giving her a drink of water. He said to her, 'Oh Sarah, what have you taken?' Dowie denied seeing her drinking from a bottle, but said that Scholes had seen her take the poison. She told the jury, 'The deceased and myself had our suppers together and were just as comfortable as usual.'

One of the jurors asked Dowie whether she had threatened to poison Sarah Scholes if she did not leave the house. Dowie denied this. The coroner questioned whether or not she was aware of the prussic acid in the house, and she told him that she did not know of it. Dowie was also interrogated about Sarah Scholes' state of mind, but she claimed there was no sign that Mrs Scholes was in any way low spirited. Another juror asked her if it was true that Scholes had killed a dog using the same poison, and Dowie admitted that it was true. She then categorically denied that Scholes had told her he would marry her if anything happened to his wife. Laconically, she told the courtroom, 'I tried to go away several times but could not, I could not forget him.'

Another witness, Samuel Healey, claimed he had known Dowie for about twelve months and that she expected to marry Scholes once his wife was no longer around. Dowie was brought back to the stand, where she denied ever saying such a thing to Healey. Once again, Healey took the stand, asserting that the relationship between the three in question was under such pressure that there were frequent quarrels, which had been heard throughout the neighbourhood.

Once more, the courtroom became silent when the husband of the deceased woman gave his evidence. He confirmed that she was his wife, saying that they had been married about fourteen years and she was aged 43. He told the coroner that he had known Dowie for about two years and had kept her for six months, before his wife suggested that she come to live with them. He confirmed that Dowie had gone to Scotland and that he had made an agreement to separate from his wife. The maintenance arrangements had been agreed by an attorney. Dowie came back to live with him in the marital home during May and, at that time, he was separated from his wife. His wife then returned and since that time, they had all lived together quite amicably. When questioned by the coroner, Scholes explained, 'My wife seemed right enough and though I have no doubt that it would hurt her feelings, she consented to it.'

On the night his wife died, he claimed to have been out from 10 a.m. to 5 p.m. He then went out again at 7 p.m. and returned at 10 p.m., going to bed about half an hour later. Scholes told the incredulous jury that nothing unpleasant had occurred. He said that he had gone to bed and his wife had come into his room. He had simply fallen asleep. At around 12 o'clock, he awoke to the sound of Dowie and his wife talking, and he asked her why she was not in bed. She told him that she wanted to sit up and refused to go into the bed she shared with Dowie. His wife had then ran out the room and returned with a bottle. He was, apparently, unaware that there was prussic acid in the house, although he knew he had used some when he poisoned a dog with it the previous May. On that occasion, he had bought two pennyworth (about half a teaspoon). According to Scholes, there was no label on the bottle and he told the inquiry he had broken the empty bottle after giving the prussic acid to the dog.

When asked by the coroner about the emotional condition of his wife, he said that she had been in good spirits, that about seven or eight years before he met Dowie she had spoken of suicide, but that was in the past. A juror asked him how his wife felt about sharing the house with Dowie. Scholes spoke of how his wife had returned to him two months ago, asking him to 'turn Margaret out', but he had replied that he would turn neither of them out. The coroner rebuked him, saying that if he had acted as he ought to have done, he would have turned Dowie away: 'Your wife had the only moral claim on you.' Scholes told the court that from the moment Dowie had come to the house, his wife had ceased to sleep with him. He claimed not to remember saying to Dowie that he would marry her if anything happened to his wife.

Dowie was put on the stand once again and re-questioned about exactly who had fetched her from the 'house of ill-fame' on Union Street. She told them that it was actually Scholes who had fetched her, but his wife was with him and had said to her, 'Come away home with us lass.' She gave that as the reason for the resumption of their strange domestic arrangements.

Two more neighbours were called to the stand, who gave evidence as to the state of mind of Mrs Scholes on the day of her death. Both stated that they saw nothing unusual in her manner. Dowie was called back once again to explain discrepancies in her statement but 'nothing material developed'. The coroner then told the jury that they had three questions to consider. The first was how the woman came by her death – and of this he thought that they could have no doubt. Secondly, by whom the poison was administered – whether by other persons or by herself. Thirdly, if she administered it herself, they had to identify her state of mind at the time. He then asked the jury if they had enough evidence to bring in a verdict, or if they would like to adjourn the inquest until further evidence could be sought. The jury opted for the latter and the inquest was adjourned until the following Thursday at 5 p.m.

On Thursday 22 December, the adjourned inquest was continued. Some additional information had been laid before the coroner, but it was apparently 'of little use'. Finally, after summing up all the evidence, the jury brought in the following verdict: 'The deceased died from the effects of poison; but how, or by whom administered, there is no evidence to determine.' The jury requested that the coroner severely reprimand the couple for their conduct, which in their opinion had led – if not directly then certainly indirectly – to the poor woman's death. A great many persons from the Scholes' neighbourhood were waiting to hear the verdict and he requested the protection of the police, as he was afraid of being assaulted.

Death of a Young Sweetheart

The Execution of Thomas Malkin, 1849

Suspect:	*Thomas Malkin*
Age:	*17*
Charge:	*Wilful Murder*
Sentence:	*Execution*

Traditionally young people met and fell in love either at church or at work; but in the next case, it is unclear where the two young people originally met, as they attended the same church, as well as working for the same employer. However, they were only going out with each other for just over a year, before the affair ceased. It was then that what should have been an innocent episode of young romance escalated into cold-blooded murder.

Esther Inman was only 15 years of age when she started work at the flax-spinning mill of Messrs W.B. Holdsworth and Co. of Hunslet, near Leeds. At the same time, she attended and sang in the choir of the Primitive Methodist church at Hunslet. It was at this point that she met Thomas Malkin, aged 17, who was a wood turner by trade and employed at the same spinning mill. The liaison was accepted by her family and friends, and the young couple enjoyed each other's company for over a year. So it was to everyone's surprise when Esther told Malkin that she didn't want to see him any more. Instead of accepting the situation gracefully, he became more and more obsessed with her refusal.

On the morning of Sunday, 8 October 1848, Esther and Malkin had attended church separately and later that night, he arrived unexpectedly at her house. Esther had been to see her younger sister, who was in service at Kirkstall, and had returned home at around 9.50 p.m. She lived at the house of her stepfather, Thomas Watson, a tailor of Hunslet, along with her mother and elder sister. The family also had other visitors at the house that night; a mother and daughter, Ann and Mary Ann Smith. As Mary Ann left the house, she saw Malkin hanging around and he told her that he wanted to see Esther for a moment. Esther had already taken off her boots, prior to retiring, but she patiently put them on again and went outside to talk to him. At the same time both Smiths left the house and Thomas Watson saw them off, all three clearly seeing Esther talking to Malkin at the back gate. Esther had only been outside about five minutes when her stepfather heard her cry out and, rushing outside, found her laid prostrate on the garden. He picked her up in his arms and carried her indoors. She cried out, 'Lord help me!' and 'Lord have mercy on me!' Laying her down, he saw that Malkin had cut her throat in two places and she had defence wounds up her arms. Indeed, one of the blows to her arm had been so vicious that Malkin's dagger had broken, and the point of the blade was still embedded in her flesh. In the folds of her right-hand sleeve was also found another dagger. Several witnesses reported seeing Malkin talking to Esther by the garden gate and hearing her cry out as he run out of the garden. A surgeon was called and arrived at the same time as the police constable; however, within the hour she was dead.

A search was made for Malkin, but nothing more was seen or heard of him that night. PC Stead later told the magistrates that he had looked for Malkin at his home, at his sister's house, at his brother's residence and in other places, but he had been unable to find him. It was thought by the police that he had probably committed suicide by throwing himself into the River Aire.

News of the murder had spread throughout Hunslet and Leeds, and the following evening the murderer was spotted. Mr John Dudley, of Greenwood Street, saw Malkin in Vicar Lane, Leeds, at around 10 p.m. He went straight to the police office and informed Inspector Child. Immediately, Child and Dudley went to the area and found Malkin. They asked him his name and he replied that he did not know. Child took him to the police station, where he was arrested for the wilful murder of Esther Inman. When asked if he had anything to say, Malkin just shook his head. The next morning he was brought before magistrates – including the mayor, Mr F. Garbutt Esq. and J. Holdforth Esq. – charged with the murder. He was remanded to the following day, until the inquest could be heard. Several witnesses gave evidence to the coroner, confirming that the couple had been seen together before the attack.

(Before Mr. BARON PLATT.)

MURDER AT LEEDS.

This morning the Court was crowded to hear the trial of THOMAS MALKIN (17), charged with the wilful murder of Esther Inman. at Hunslet, near Leeds. The indictment charged the prisoner with having, at the parish of Leeds, on the 8th of October, feloniously, wilfully, and of his malice aforethought, assaulted Esther Inman, and with a dagger, which he then and there held in his right hand, did feloniously stab, strike, and thrust the said Esther Inman on the right side of her chest, then and there, and thereby giving her one mortal wound, of the length of one inch, and of the depth of four inches, of which the said Esther Inman instantly died; and that he (the prisoner) by these means did kill and murder the said Esther Inman. There was another count in the indictment charging the prisoner with stabbing the deceased on the right breast. To this indictment he pleaded Not Guilty, in a firm tone of voice.

Mr. HALL, Mr. HILL, and Mr. WHEELHOUSE appeared for the prosecution; Mr. OVEREND and Mr. JOHNSTONE defended the prisoner.

After the Jury had been sworn and charged,

Mr. HALL rose and said,—May it please your Lordship; Gentlemen of the Jury, the prisoner at the bar stands charged before you, on the finding of the Grand Jury, and also of the Coroner's inquest, with the wilful murder of Esther Inman by stabbing her with a dagger. It is unnecessary for me to invite your painful and anxious attention to this case, both as regards the interests of the public, and the interests of the party charged—of the public, because it is a question that concerns the personal safety of all—of the party charged, because the nature of the punishment which follows conviction is irrevocable. Though this is a case which depends almost entirely on circumstancial evidence, it is a case of not much complication. It is a case which derives a melancholy—I might almost say a romantic—interest from the relation in which the prisoner stood to the young woman, whose death the prisoner is now charged with causing. Gentlemen, the deceased, Esther Inman, a girl between sixteen and seventeen years of age, lived at Hunslet, near Leeds, with her step-father, Thomas Watson, a tailor there. The prisoner, a boy between seventeen and eighteen, lived also at Hunslet with his father, who is a wood turner with [...] [...] years in that capacity [...] ly respectable

A newspaper account of the murder by Thomas Malkin.

On Wednesday 11 October, Malkin was brought before the magistrates at Leeds, and the witness' testimony was heard once more. The magistrate summed up the evidence and, within the space of half an hour, the jury found him guilty, and the magistrate ordered him to take his trial at the next Assizes. Malkin appeared before the Leeds Assizes on Wednesday, 20 December 1848, in front of Mr Baron Platts. The courtroom was crowded, as much interest had been raised in the case. Malkin was heard to plead 'not guilty' in a firm tone of voice. One witness, John Raynor, told the court that he saw the couple move away from the gate and further into the garden. He stated that when he saw them, Malkin had his left hand on the breast of the young woman and his right hand in his pocket, as if he was about to strike her with his dagger. He called to Malkin, telling him to leave Esther alone, and she re-assured him that everything was alright. At this point he walked away. Within a few seconds, he heard the girl scream and cry out 'murder!' at which he quickly returned to see another witness by the girl's side. He watched helplessly whilst Malkin ran out of the gate and towards his parent's house. He then saw Malkin's mother come out of her own house, as she ran to the house of the dying girl.

The next person to give evidence was the stepfather of the dead girl, Thomas Watson. He told the court that he had married Esther's mother about twelve months previously. The girl had been 16 years, 6 months and just a few days old at her death. According to Watson's account, Esther had tried to remain on friendly terms with Malkin and always appeared willing enough to talk to him when he turned up at the house. Watson told the judge that he had seen them together at 11 p.m. on the night before the murder. On the fateful day, he described how his stepdaughter had gone out after dinner to see her sister: 'She was at that time more cheerful than I had ever seen her,' he lamented. Watson described the night's events, only being interrupted by Superintendent James producing the murder weapon for him to identify. The weapon was described as resembling a narrow, pointed chisel. He said that his daughter also had a dagger, which was produced in court. This dagger was much shorter than the weapon that caused the murder. Watson explained that he had taken the smaller dagger away from her about five or six weeks previously. He had not said anything to his stepdaughter about it, but had merely locked it away in a drawer. When questioned, Watson revealed that the drawer was sometimes locked and at other times left open.

A surgeon, Mr Richard Pullen of Hunslet, gave evidence on what he had found in the post-mortem of the girl's body. He commented that her organs were in an extremely healthy state and gave his opinion that the cause of death was from the wounds she had received.

Both the Smiths gave evidence to corroborate the events already outlined. Mary Ann described how Malkin had questioned Esther about where she had been but, as far as she could hear, this was done in a friendly manner. She said, 'Esther came out readily to see Malkin and he seemed pleased to see her.' Esther's sister, Elizabeth, spoke of how she had seen Malkin at the chapel on the evening of the murder, although he did not stay until the end. She spoke of her sister being called outside by Malkin and hearing her cry out, 'He has stuck me!' Elizabeth was the one who found the smaller dagger in her sister's pocket prior to the attack, and had given it to her stepfather for safekeeping.

William James, the Superintendent of Leeds Police, described the search for Malkin on the night of the murder. It had extended to lodging houses and derelict sheds, but the following evening he was informed that Malkin was in custody. He went to the police cells to interview him, but the prisoner refused to respond to his questioning. Soon after, Mary Ann Smith came in and, going up to Malkin, stated, 'That's Thomas Malkin!' and the prisoner replied, 'Yes, I know her.' When she accused him of the murder and the encounter beforehand, Malkin denied it, saying, 'I did not send you to fetch her out. I was not there at all. I know nothing about it.' Superintendent James told the court that the prisoner had tried to act 'stupid' at first, but had dropped that act when Mary Ann Smith challenged him.

Another witness, John Watson, said that after the murder, he saw Malkin go to his own father's house. Being an acquaintance of the family, he followed him inside, where he saw Malkin's father, mother and brother in the house. He described Malkin as 'white looking in the face'. His brother said to him, 'Tom, what's thou been doing?' and he first replied, 'Nay, nowt,' but then admitted, 'Yes I have, I have done her job at last.' His mother cried out, 'Tom, thou surely haven't, has thou?' He answered, 'If you won't believe me, you must go and see for yourself.' His mother quickly got her shawl and went out.

Later, as Watson left Malkin and his brother in the house, he saw Malkin's mother coming back to the house. She held her arms out wide and her hair was dishevelled down her shoulders; she was crying and screaming. A workmate of Malkin's, Joseph Hobson, said that six months before Esther died, he had said to Malkin, 'Tom you and Esther have been fratching [quarrelling] haven't you?' Malkin had replied, 'Aye and I will kill her.' When the magistrate asked Hobson what his response to this had been, he stated that he didn't take it seriously and thought no more about it.

Another workmate, Thomas Wylde, told of Malkin asking him for a piece of steel to use as 'a picker' at his work, about three months before Esther's death. After this, Malkin brought it back and asked him to flatten it for him, which he did. When the murder weapon was produced in court, he identified it as the piece of metal he had flattened, but he noted that it had subsequently been ground at the edges. Two other witnesses claimed to have seen Malkin with this piece of steel, which he had sharpened himself.

The defence counsel, Mr Overend, rose to make his speech on behalf of the prisoner. He described the relationship between the two lovers. They had been in constant communication with each other right up to the night before the murder. Malkin had been described as a boy of respectable parents and not 'an abandoned character', as had been reported in the newspapers. Mr Overend asked the jury, 'Is it possible that such a young man of such good character and of such habits should wish to kill the object of his love?' Overend stated that the way in which the girl had met her death was a mystery and it was merely circumstantial testimony that framed Malkin as her murderer. There were no witnesses who had actually seen Malkin strike the girl with the weapon. From the evidence, he suggests, it might have been a case of self-destruction, as there was clear verification that she had carried around her own dagger. He told the jury, 'The prisoner is entitled to a verdict and the jury must think long and hard about it. If you truly believe that an attack was carried out by this young man in the heat of the moment, then you should return a verdict of manslaughter.'

The judge summed up all the evidence for the jury and they brought in a verdict of guilty, but with a recommendation for mercy due to Malkin's very young age. The judge put on the black cap and speaking very solemnly told him:

Thomas Malkin, you have been convicted by a jury of the crime of murder. Yours is a case certainly exciting great commiseration, if a man committing so heinous a crime could be commiserated with; but that is impossible. Murder is of such diabolical malignity, that it is necessary to be punished when a party is convicted, and it is improper that mercy should be extended to those who have committed it. It is quite impossible for me to hold out any hopes of mercy to you. It seems to me that your case, although it has moved all who have heard it, is not one to which I can extend any hope. It is true you began life with respectability – but you forgot to curb that malicious tendency of the human heart which, if not curbed, leads to every kind of malignant mischief.

Throughout the trial, Malkin had seemed indifferent to his fate and showed no signs of contrition. Two days before his execution, on Thursday 4 January, he confessed to the prison chaplain that he had in fact murdered his sweetheart and that the verdict was just. When asked to justify himself, he spoke of being angry when she had rejected his advances. Malkin told the chaplain that he had, indeed, been plotting to murder Esther for four or five weeks before he plucked up the courage to do it. Although he was unable to explain why he was so determined that she would die, Malkin displayed to the chaplain true signs of penitence and a spiritual awareness of his position. He was brought out onto the scaffold on Saturday, 6 January 1849. There was an audible gasp from the crowd because he looked so young, and a vast concourse of faces watched him as the executioner pulled the bolt. After a few moments he was dead. At Armley Gaol, his body would have been removed through a gateway before being buried in the paupers' graveyard, which is now under the car park.

The death of both these young people was a tragedy, as neither appeared to have possessed the good judgment that comes with maturity. However, there do seem to be some factors that still need explaining. Why did Esther carry a

knife around with her, for example? Had Malkin threatened to kill her? If that was the case, why did the couple appear to be on such friendly terms after the break up? She had been described by her stepfather as a 'short-tempered girl', which the defence used to their advantage in trying to prove that she killed herself. As with so many of these cases, we will never know.

The gateway through which the bodies of executed felons were taken to be buried in the paupers' graveyard.

A typical cell at Leeds Town Hall, where Malkin could have been held whilst the police interrogated him.

SOLVED

Solved by a Pawn Ticket

The Case of Charles Normington, 1859

Suspect:	*Charles Normington*
Age:	*17*
Charge:	*Murder*
Sentence:	*Execution*

During the nineteenth century, it was common practice to pawn items of clothing, jewellery or furniture in order to obtain money, until the item could be redeemed. Pawnshops could be found on almost every corner of Leeds's streets, and it was common practice amongst the working classes to pawn items at the beginning of the week to redeem them after payday. In some cases, if the item was a valuable piece of jewellery or a watch, the pawn ticket itself was sold for a small sum and the person buying it would then redeem the item, hopefully making a small profit out of the deal. In August 1859, such a transaction led to a brutal attack on an old man.

On Saturday, 6 August 1859, Mr Richard Broughton left his home to go into Leeds town centre to conduct some business. The gentleman, who was a retired porter, was aged 67 and lived at Rose Cottage Yard, Roundhay. He was later found beaten so badly that he died the following day. Before he died, Broughton stated that he had been robbed by two men. Two boys found the body and one of them reported seeing a man wearing a blue smock, leaning against a fence, just before they found the body. When the boy attempted to speak to the man, he ran away. Broughton's stolen watch had been pawned on the day after the murder at a shop owned by Mr Barras of Dyer Lane, in Leeds. A description of the seller was given to the Leeds police. Two men, William Appleby and Walter Bearden, were apprehended after the robbery, named as being the two men who had been seen in a field shortly after the body of Mr Broughton had been found.

On Saturday 3 September, the magistrates found that there was not enough evidence against Appleby to further detain him, and so he was discharged. On 6 September, a report was heard that a man, James Smales, had tried to redeem the watch belonging to the murdered man; he was then arrested and taken before the Chief Constable at Leeds, where he claimed to have been given the ticket by Charlie Normington for 5s at Castleton, a few days previously. A description of Normington, who was only 17 years old, was given and a £25 reward was offered for his arrest.

Whilst at Castleton, Normington had lodged with a woman named Mrs Dixon, and she told the police that she had seen him washing a handkerchief and a shirt which appeared to have blood on it. He had left the shirt behind when he disappeared from his lodgings the same day. A stick found near the body of the murdered man was, when examined, found to have blood on it and was identified as being one which Normington had owned for several weeks before the murder. The next day, Normington was arrested in Sheffield by Leeds' Chief Constable Mr English, who had disguised himself as a collier. He was brought back to Leeds and charged with the murder of the old man. Normington claimed his innocence and stated that he had bought the pawn ticket the day after the murder, on 7 August, from an Irish man he had met at Hunslet toll bar, who had walked part of the way with him. He had bought the ticket for sixpence.

Normington was brought into court at Leeds on Tuesday 6 September, along with Bearden. Both men were remanded for three days while further enquiries were made. The trial was resumed on Friday 9 September, throughout which Normington appeared to take little interest in the evidence, seemingly unconcerned by the proceedings. However, once the court had been adjourned and Normington was pushing through the crowded corridor leading out of the court, he told one of the constables that he was going to 'tell all about it before he had done'. He then asked to speak to Mr English. He was taken into a police office, where the Chief Constable attended on him with the clerk to the magistrates, Mr Barr. Normington made a full confession to Mr English, stating that he had been present when the murder was committed, although he was not on his own. He gave the name of another man called Pollard, who he said had actually attacked Mr Broughton. Nevertheless, the most damning evidence against Normington was the stick with which Mr Broughton had been attacked – the stick he had already identified as his own.

As his trial continued the following day, he was described as being 'round shouldered, strongly built and bow legged'. He had 'a round, full face with a small mole on it', and 'light-brown hair which curled a little on each side'. Bearden was in the dock with him, but was quickly found not guilty and told to stand down. Normington was asked if he had anything to say and replied with a statement to the effect that on the night of the murder, he had been pulling down his trousers to go to the toilet when the old man passed him. Next he heard the sounds of Pollard attacking the old man and then both men ran off. Normington had asked Pollard if he had killed the old man, and he shook his head but told him that there was some blood on the old man's head. He told Normington that he had thrown the stick away and that there was no need for him to be frightened, 'so long as it's me what's done it'.

A search was made for the man, Pollard, and he was eventually found, but quickly eliminated as a suspect when it was discovered that he had been in Kirkdale Prison, near Liverpool, at the time of the attack. Normington was found guilty and was sent to take his trial at the York Assizes. On the journey there, he showed no compassion for the deed, but rather a curiosity about what might happen on the scaffold. As the train headed towards York, he asked his companion about how thick the rope used for hanging felons was. He asked, 'Is it as thick as a pit rope?' to which his companion replied that it was. On reaching York, he was put into a cab and within a few minutes he was lodged in a cell at the castle.

The trial started on 15 December 1859 at 9 a.m. and continued until 5 p.m. in the evening. The prisoner caused a stir when he came into the prison, due to his small stature, being only 4ft 8¾ins in height and looking much younger than his 17 years. In court, the prosecution outlined the case, stating that on Saturday 6 August, Mr Broughton had left home around 4.45 p.m. in order to buy some food for his ducks. In his possession, he had a German silver pocket watch and a florin. He had not gone far when, in pausing to climb over a stile, he was attacked by two men. Two blows were sufficient to render him insensible, but three more blows were inflicted on him, fracturing his skull. The two men then ransacked his pockets and took the watch, although the florin was overlooked. Despite his injuries, the old man had got to his feet and staggered down to the

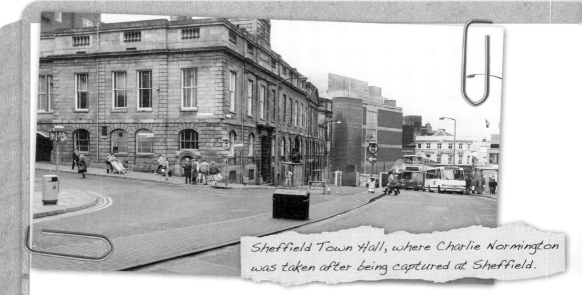

Sheffield Town Hall, where Charlie Normington was taken after being captured at Sheffield.

Solved by a Pawn Ticket

bottom of the field, where he met a person who went to help him. He kept repeating, 'Two men, two men...' Incredibly this brave old man, with the assistance of his rescuer, returned home and a surgeon was sent for. Mr Hey, the surgeon, arrived between 8 p.m. and 9 p.m. and attended to the old man who was, by then, insensible. He died at 1.40 a.m. on the following morning.

Normington's defence, Mr C. Foster, maintained that his client was innocent of the murder, but guilty of pawning the watch of the dead man. However, the evidence against Normington was too strong and the jury took only fifteen minutes to find him guilty. As the judge donned the black cap, there was a heart rending shriek from a woman, later identified as Normington's mother. The sound echoed throughout the courtroom, and she had to be physically restrained and removed. On hearing the outcome of the case, the prisoner, who had kept a calm demeanour throughout the trial, collapsed into the arms of York Castle's deputy governor, Mr Green.

When Normington was put in the condemned cell, he became extremely upset and started to cry. As a result of his distress, he was visited by Mr Green, who advised him to make full use of the time he had left to write out a true confession. He told Mr Green that he had indeed killed the old man, and that he had hit him several times, until he fell on the ground. He still maintained that he was not alone and the other unnamed man had kicked Broughton whilst he was down. His confession stated that he had not known the other man until the day of the murder and didn't know his name. He stated that after the attack on the old man, his companion opened the waistcoat, but it was Normington who had taken out the watch. He said that he had met his companion the following day at 9 a.m. near the Marsh Lane station, in order to pawn the watch. They had gone into three pawnshops before successfully pawning the watch, and he had given the man 3s and kept the remainder for himself. They had then parted. Normington wrote that he had not seen the man since.

The next day, after writing out his confession, Normington was visited by his mother at the castle and she also begged him to tell the truth. He replied, 'I have; I have told Mr Green all about it.' Mr Green, who was present at this interview, confirmed that he had a written confession which the boy had signed.

Whilst in York Castle Prison, Normington dictated a series of letters while one of the wardens wrote them out for him. It had been reported that he had spent most of his life with his mother in Leeds whilst his father lived in Bradford. The couple had parted due to his father refusing to put up with the profligate life that his son had led. The letters indicate the strength of the condemned man's religious feelings. The one to his mother is particularly heart-rending:

York Castle, 20 December 1859

My dear mother,
I send you these few lines and I sincerely hope they will find you in good health. I am glad to tell you that I am quite well and my mind is quite easy; and I can assure you that I do not fear my fate, for I put all my trust in the Lord Jesus Christ. I hope, dear Mother, that you will not fret, but pray for me, and believe me I have quite resigned myself and do not dread the hour so fast approaching. I pray the Lord to give me strength here and peace hereafter. Therefore, dear mother, do not fret for me. I can assure you, I feel very happy in my mind and hope and believe that I shall soon be in everlasting happiness and rest, for believe me, I fear nothing, trusting entirely in the Lord. I hope you will pray unto Him, and that you will be saved, and enjoy eternal happiness. This, dear mother, is my sincere prayer for you and it is hoped we shall meet again in the Kingdom of Heaven, where we shall be far happier than here in the world of trouble. I think of all of my friends, and pray for you all and hope you will all do the same for me.

I remain, dear Mother,
Your affectionate son,

CHARLES NORMINGTON

The hanging scene, which attracted crowds of people wanting to see prisoners being executed.

Solved by a Pawn Ticket

In a second letter, written to his father, Normington castigated him for leaving his mother and himself to fend for themselves. He wrote the letter on 28 December and in it he tells his father that he has just had a last meeting with his mother:

You know what a great sin you have committed by leaving my mother and your family to the wide world in the way you did. Dear Father, I could die now content if I thought you and mother would live together again. I pray for you, and I forgive you, and I hope God will forgive you.

Two more letters were written before the day of his execution arrived. There was another to his mother, asking her once again to pray for him. The second was to his aunt and uncle, asking them to do the same.

On Saturday, 31 December 1859, Normington was visited in his cell by the Reverend Thomas Myers and the prison chaplain. The two ministers spent the last hour that Normington would have on this earth by his side. They read part of the scriptures to him and sung hymns, to which the warders joined in. Just before noon, the sacrament was administered to him. The hangman, Askern, then entered the cell and pinioned the young man's arms behind his back before he was led out to the scaffold. It was reported that Normington walked onto the scaffold with a firm step and appeared composed as he knelt to say his last prayers. Before a crowd of between 9,000 and 10,000 people, Normington called out, 'Lord, have mercy on my soul.' Askern then adjusted the fatal noose and withdrew the bolt. It was reported that his struggles were not severe and lasted only two minutes. These kinds of executions were a celebrated day out for many people of the Victorian period. Although horrific to modern-day minds, notorious murderers, like William Palmer, would attract crowds of spectators, men and woman alike.

SOLVED

Attempted Murder of a Shopkeeper

The Trial of John Kenworthy, 1860

Suspect:	*John Kenworthy*
Age:	*25*
Charge:	*Attempted Murder*
Sentence:	*Fifteen Years' Transportation*

This next case is another that leaves us with more questions than answers. We know that a shopkeeper was attacked, but the motive is difficult to ascertain, as it was evidently not for gain.

In the nineteenth century, it was quite easy to go into business as a shopkeeper. You just filled up the windows with some of the stock for sale and opened the front door to customers. One of the drawbacks, however, was that customers tended to call on you at all hours of the day and night. It was while dealing with an early morning customer that this shopkeeper almost met his end.

Stephen Lupton, aged 29, was a single man who owned a shop, which was situated on the corner of Oldforth Street and Cross Street, New Wortley, near Leeds. The shop was typical of its time; it had the shop part at the front of the house and his living area at the back.

Twenty-five-year-old John Kenworthy was a married man and lived in Campbell Street, which was about 300 yards from Lupton's shop. The shop sold basic provisions, such as groceries, castor oil and a few drugs. On Monday 8 October 1860, Lupton was woken at five o'clock by someone banging on his door. He opened his bedroom window and saw Kenworthy. He shouted down to him, asking him what he wanted, and Kenworthy shouted back that he wanted some castor oil. Patiently, Lupton put on his trousers, socks and slippers, and went downstairs to let him into the shop. As he lit a candle in order to see the transactions, he asked Kenworthy why he wanted castor oil at that time of the morning, enquiring whether his wife was ill. (Kenworthy's wife worked for Lupton as a cleaner two days a week.) Kenworthy told him that the castor oil was needed for a woman 'up the street', but he did not give her name. He said he had tried to wake another shopkeeper that morning, but to no avail. Kenworthy gave Lupton a small bottle and asked him how much castor oil he could get in it. Lupton told him that it would probably hold about two ounces and he went through to the house section and filled the bottle. Going back into the shop, he put the bottle onto the counter and then Kenworthy asked him for some mint lozenges. Lupton told him they were a penny an ounce, and Kenworthy requested two ounces. Lupton weighed out the mint lozenges and gave them to Kenworthy. To his astonishment, Kenworthy then asked for two ounces of arrowroot, two penny worth of nitre and a pound of pearl barley. This patient man turned to get the items and, being about 2 yards away from Kenworthy, felt a heavy blow on the crown of his head. He fell to his knees and almost immediately felt a second blow. During the attack, Kenworthy had not spoken a word to him.

The candle blew out as Lupton staggered to his feet, and the two men struggled together in the dark. The pair, who by now were at the bottom of the stairs leading to the bedrooms, scuffled together for some time. Suddenly, Kenworthy sank his teeth into Lupton's nose, who retaliated by biting his opponent's finger. Finally, Lupton managed to break free from Kenworthy and, bleeding profusely and utterly exhausted, managed to pull himself into the shop section of the house. By now, Kenworthy had run upstairs and Lupton heard him moving from room to room, as if he was ransacking the place. Lupton tried to open the shop door to get into the street, but was unable to, so he went towards the door which led into a small warehouse, where he kept his stock. Almost dropping down the three or four steps from the warehouse into the street, he managed to crawl outside. He shouted 'Murder!' at the top of his voice and Mrs Mary Ann Horner, a widow whose house adjoined the shop, came outside. Seeing the distressed man she rushed to help him up.

At that point the door of the shop opened and Kenworthy stood there. She told him, 'You are the man that has done this and you will pay dearly for it.' Kenworthy shouted something back in return, but she didn't hear what it was.

She then tried to help the injured man, who by now was covered in so much blood that she couldn't actually see where he had been injured. Another neighbour, Mr Thackeray, came to help and the two of them managed to get Lupton back into the house and seated on a chair. The two neighbours were horrified at the amount of blood in the shop, the parlour, the hallway and the warehouse. When they cleaned the poor man up, they saw the wound on his head, which appeared to have been made by a very sharp implement. Whilst searching the shop section, they found a hatchet under a chair, which was later proved to belong to Kenworthy.

A surgeon, Mr W. Scott, was sent for and, on arrival, he ordered that the injured man be sent to bed. On shaving Lupton's head, he found five separate scalp wounds, several superficial scratches on his face and a mark on his nose. On the crown of his head was there a fracture on the left-hand side. Three of the wounds on his head had been inflicted with a blunt-edged instrument, used with great force. Mr W. Scott then inspected the hatchet, which was found to have blood on it as well as hairs from Lupton's scalp. Kenworthy was also examined, and a wound on his thumb was discovered, closely resembling a bite mark.

A constable, PC John Scott, was called and took the details from the victim and the neighbours when he arrived. He went to arrest Kenworthy later that morning, who claimed that he was innocent and denied being anywhere near the shop. He was taken to the police station and placed in a cell, where unruly prisoners could be tied to a seat by their manacles. Kenworthy made a statement and, following this, PC Scott went to Kenworthy's mother's house at Beeston Royds where, armed with a search warrant, he investigated the house. Kenworthy had told him that morning he had been to his mother's house, and a lodger, George Gibbons, had given him a fresh coat and waistcoat before leaving the house to go home. Gibbons told PC Scott that Kenworthy was about to move back in with his mother, as it was nearer to his place of employment. He added that when he saw him and lent him the coat, he seemed quite 'normal'.

Scott found the discarded waistcoat, which still had spots of blood on it, hidden in Kenworthy's mother's bed, underneath the mattress. The fustian waistcoat was identified by the tailor named Paget at Wakefield, as being the one he made for Kenworthy. PC Scott also found a sign of burnt clothing in one of the bedrooms in the mother's house. Scott then went to the house where Kenworthy lived with his wife, where he found a torn collar, a hat and a bloody towel. Kenworthy's wife told him that she had already pawned a pair of trousers and a hat which Kenworthy had been wearing that day. She had taken them to the shop of a pawnbroker on Whittington Street. The trousers were recovered and they were found to have bloodstains on them too, as was his hat.

Meanwhile, Kenworthy was taken to be identified by Lupton, who stated that this was indeed his attacker. Mrs Horner, also present, identified him as the man who was last seen running out of the shop as well. She told him, 'You're the villain. I told you that you would suffer for this.' In front of both Lupton and Mrs Horner, PC Scott said to him, 'Now you see what you are charged with, what have you to say for yourself?' But insolently, Kenworthy persisted in his denial. When Scott returned back to the police station, he found that one of the cleaners, a Mrs Jane Blanchard, had found a bent, bloodstained knife whilst sweeping the charge room. The knife appeared to have been kicked out of sight under a chair, in the same room the prisoner had been placed after he had been charged. The reason for the robbery was unclear, as a watch and some money were found in Lupton's bedroom untouched. The *Leeds Mercury* suggested that the prisoner might have had some questions around his wife's chastity, and the reason for ransacking the bedroom was not for plunder, but to find any evidence to his wife's supposed infidelity.

On Thursday, 20 December 1860, Kenworthy appeared at the Assizes before Mr Justice Hill, charged with the attempted murder of Stephen Lupton on Monday 8 October. The prisoner was defended by Mr Maule; Mr Foster and Mr Hanney were for the prosecution. The first witness to take the stand was Lupton, whose head was still bandaged from the ordeal. He re-iterated the circumstances of the vicious attack and positively identified Kenworthy as the attacker.

Mrs Horner followed him in the witness box and told the jury that her bedroom adjoined that of the victim, and she was awoken by the prisoner shouting to Lupton, stating that he needed some oil. She also heard Lupton get out of bed and open the front door, letting Kenworthy into the shop. She heard the scuffle, as well as a heavy fall, followed by a cry of 'Murder!' Hastily dressing, she ran out of the house to find Lupton in the street, badly injured. She also positively identified Kenworthy as the man who came out of the shop that morning. After she had given her evidence, she was praised by the judge for her courage in standing up to the attacker.

The next witness was the police inspector, Mr English, who told the court that he had twenty of his best men on the case at the time and was convinced of the prisoner's guilt. Kenworthy's employer, Mr Daniel Bazendale of the Farnley Iron Company, identified the axe used in the attack as one which had been stolen from his workplace about six months previously. He told the jury that few men had access to the stores where the axe had been kept, but Kenworthy had enjoyed that privilege. He stated that the prisoner had worked for him for almost eleven years.

However, the prisoners defence, Mr Maule, claimed that the case had too many irrelevances in it and the identification was 'shaky'. He said there was little evidence to show that the knife found at the

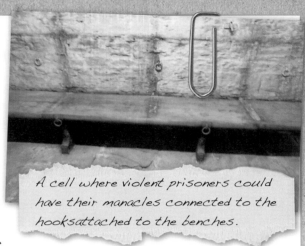

A cell where violent prisoners could have their manacles connected to the hooks attached to the benches.

police station had belonged to Kenworthy. He also claimed that the police had 'pulled to pieces' the house belonging to the prisoner's mother, where the waistcoat had been found. There was little evidence that the stains were blood, and all it proved was that it was the waistcoat he had worn on that day. He also spoke of the witnesses, claiming that on the day of the assault, the attacker was wearing a long, black coat, buttoned up to the neck. He asked, 'Where is that coat which, despite the aid of twenty police constables, has not been found?' He also questioned the identification of Kenworthy by Mr Lupton, due to the fact that the candle had been extinguished at the onset of the attack. He stated, 'With respect to Mrs Horner's recognition, I feel that she was erroneous.' He advised the jury to discount her hasty identification of the man seen coming out of the shop. Finally, he told the jury that the hatchet had not been positively identified as the one belonging to the prisoner.

The judge, Mr Justice Hill, summed up for the jury, going into each minute detail. Despite Mr Maule's claims, he expressed the opinion that there was very strong, direct evidence of the prisoner's guilt. The jury agreed and only retired for five minutes before they returned a verdict of 'guilty of wounding, with an attempt to do grievous bodily harm'. The judge then spoke to the prisoner:

You have been convicted of a crime which is almost unparalleled in its outrageous character. The evidence against you was clear and cogent and you know yourself in your own conscience whether you intended to murder the man. The jury has taken a lenient view of the case, but they have felt compelled to convict you of wounding, with intent to do bodily harm. I should be wanting in my duty to the public and every individual who now hears my voice, if I did not pass on you the most severe sentence.

The witness box where Mrs Horner gave her evidence.

Mrs Kenworthy watched her husband descend the steps from the dock to the cells after he was sentenced to transportation for fifteen years.

In a very loud, cold voice, Mr Justice Hill sentenced John Kenworthy to the maximum sentence of fifteen years' transportation. Kenworthy showed no emotion as he was led from the dock. His wife, who was present in court, was in tears as she saw her husband descend down the stairs to start his sentence. John Kenworthy was one of 290 convicts who sailed on the convict ship *Norwood* on 13 March 1862, to spend fifteen years in Western Australia. This case is very intriguing and begs the question, was it just a matter of greed? Certainly there is no evidence that any items of value were taken from the shop. What did Kenworthy get out of it? Were the reasons for the attack more sinister? We know that Mrs Kenworthy worked for Lupton twice a week, and he was a single man who was obviously in a better financial position than her husband. Was there some romantic involvement of which the court was unaware, or was it just a case of pure malice? Did Kenworthy go to the shop that morning in a fit of jealous rage to try to kill the man he suspected of seducing his wife? One thing for certain is that Kenworthy had fifteen years to mull over the true reasons for his crime.

SOLVED

The Wanton Wife

The Acquittal of John Dearden, 1872

Suspect:	*John Dearden*
Age:	*57*
Charge:	*Wilful Murder*
Sentence:	*Not Guilty*

In July 1872, a man named John Dearden lived with his second wife, Minnie, at a temperance hotel on Old Hall Street, Burmantofts, Leeds, which he had bought out of his savings from being a sea captain. The hotel had formerly been a very old hall, which had been separated into three dwellings.

Dearden had been married before and had several children to his first wife. Aged 57, he had found love with a much younger woman – half his age – and married her at Hull. The couple had lived together for three years, having resided at Killinghurst near Sheffield before moving to Leeds. The marriage had been good and he was apparently very fond of his wife, but then things started to change. In the few weeks leading up to her murder on Wednesday 12 July, she had begun staying out all night, and her husband heard that on one occasion she had spent a night playing dominoes with two men.

For some weeks, her husband had been making enquiries and it seems that Minnie had started co-habiting with a former paramour, with whom she had lived before her marriage to Dearden. Matters came to a head when she left home on the night of Monday 8 July, taking a sum of money out of their savings, and did not return until 9 p.m. on Wednesday evening. Dearden had searched the local hostelries without finding her, and when she returned the couple began to argue. The neighbours, hearing the loud voices, kept to their own houses but then a shot rang out. A man named Benjamin Foxcroft, who lived in another part of the old hall, went to the hotel, where he found Mrs Dearden lying on a sofa at one side of a table and Dearden seated at the other side. In his hand he held a revolver, and, as Foxcroft entered, he held the gun up to his own head. Foxcroft grabbed at the gun and wrestled the weapon away from Dearden. He told Foxcroft, 'I took the revolver out of my pocket and threw it on the table and it went off and shot her.'

A surgeon, Mr Holmes, was called and he found the woman still alive, but bleeding from the temple. Burn marks around the wound showed that the gun had been held close to her head when she was shot. He did everything he could to make her comfortable but, despite his ministrations, she died at 2 a.m. the following day.

Dearden was arrested later that night and taken to Marsh Lane police station by PC Cuthbertson, charged with the unlawful shooting of his wife with an attempt to murder her. Inspector Williamson received the revolver and, on inspection, found it to have five bullets left in the six-bullet chamber. On Thursday 11 July, Dearden appeared at Leeds Town Hall on a charge of wilful murder.

Foxcroft was the first witness. He revealed that he had known the couple for about five weeks, in the time they lived next door to him. He said that at around 9.20 p.m. he heard a shot and ran into the house next door, his wife close on his heels. The couple were in the sitting room of the temperance hotel. When he saw Dearden, he said to him, 'John what have you done?' He went over to Mrs Dearden and spoke to her, saying, 'It is a very bad job that you had carried on as you have done,' but she made no reply. Foxcroft took the gun away from Dearden, taking it to his own house and putting it on the top of a high cupboard. When he returned, Dearden was kneeling at the side of his wife calling her 'Minnie', but she did not reply – nor did she seem to understand that he was there.

Mrs Foxcroft attended to the dying woman whilst her husband went to find a doctor. When Dearden was arrested, and before he left the house, he said to Foxcroft, 'Benjamin I leave all in your care.' Handing him the keys of the house, he asked him to make sure the house was secure and locked up. The magistrate asked him about the relationship between Dearden and his wife during those last few days, and he told him that she had taken some money and gone out on the Monday night. He heard later that she had been seen in Leeds,

Hull Town Hall.

drinking in the company of some men. He went into Dearden's part of the house on the Tuesday, where the man had told him Minnie had not returned, and then he began to cry like a baby. Under further questioning, he said that she had been known to stay away for as long as a fortnight. Dearden was then asked if he wanted a solicitor to defend him and Mr Malcolm was appointed. At this point, the magistrate adjourned the case, as an inquest would be held on the body of Mrs Dearden later that day. Deardon was held in a cell at the Town Hall until the inquest and trial were completed.

At the inquest, the coroner, Mr Emsley, examined several witnesses and the events were corroborated. The only surprise witness was the daughter of Mr Dearden, Harriet, who was aged 14 and in service with Mr Carter of the Albion Inn, Lemon Street. She told the court that her stepmother had left her father and gone to live with another man whilst the couple lived in Sheffield. Her father had gone to get her back and all three of them had moved to Leeds five weeks previously. She and another servant, named Emma Jackson, had been at her father's house just prior to the accident, and when they had left the couple were laughing and joking. She promised her father that she would come back on Sunday for tea, and she wore a brooch which her stepmother

A typical cell door at Leeds Town Hall; notice the square hole in the door where meals could be pushed through.

had lent her when she left the house. Harriet told the coroner that Dearden had got the gun whilst he was a captain at Hull. The inquest was then adjourned to Friday 18 July. At the resumed inquest, evidence was heard from 11-year-old Louisa Scott, who cleaned for Mr and Mrs Dearden. She had gone to the house on Tuesday to find no one in, and so had returned the following evening in order to light the fire. Mrs Dearden was on the sofa in the sitting room and Dearden was in the kitchen. She had promised to pay Scott 6d for cleaning, and Dearden went to put his hands in his jacket, which was over a chair, to find the money. He then went into the sitting room saying, 'Minnie you have got my money,' and he seemed very angry. The child told the court that he was so angry, she ran out of the house, fearing that there would be an argument. She heard the shot later that night and saw people going into the Deardens' house. Mrs Parkinson, the landlady of the Fleece Inn on the High Street, Burmantofts, said that the prisoner and the deceased were drinking in her pub earlier on Wednesday. She told the coroner that Mrs Dearden had gone in at around 2 p.m. and had bought a whisky, saying that she had asked her husband to meet her there between 2 p.m. and 3 p.m. that afternoon. Shortly afterwards, her husband arrived and they sat drinking until about 7 p.m. Mrs Dearden had drunk five or six glasses of whisky; Dearden had consumed about three or four.

Henry Tinsdale, the landlord of the Woodpecker at Burmantofts, took up the story. In his account, the couple went into his pub after leaving the Fleece and had two or three glasses of whisky between them. Mary Welton, a charwoman at the Albion Inn, where their daughter Harriett was employed, stated that she had seen Mrs Dearden drinking there several times, either on her own or with other men. On the Tuesday, a week before the incident, Dearden had told her that his wife had 'gone off again'. Welton told him, 'I wouldn't bother with her any more,' and Dearden replied, 'Well, I will settle it one way or the other, because I am tired of her bad ways.' He also told her that he would break up his home and move away.

The jury retired to consider their position and came back with a guilty verdict. However, they asked for leniency, due to the great provocation suffered at the hands of his wife.

On Friday 12 July, Dearden was brought into court at Leeds Town Hall before the magistrate, Mr Bruce. The first witness was Mrs Ann Foxcroft, who described trying the help the poor woman after the shooting and Dearden's distress at what had happened. Whilst Mrs Foxcroft was in the house, she heard Dearden saying several times that he had thrown down the revolver onto the table and it had gone off accidentally. She claimed that the deceased woman smelt very strongly of alcohol. When asked by the magistrate if the pair had lived happily together, she replied that Dearden did all he could to make his wife happy. According to Mrs Foxcroft, the prisoner adored his wife and could not bear to have her out of his sight. At this point, the prisoner started to cry in the dock. She told the court that she had heard him say to his dead wife that he would give her anything if she would 'only take up and be steady'.

Mr Henry Holmes, the surgeon, spoke about trying to help the injured woman. He got a sponge and wiped the wound, which he observed had penetrated right into the brain. He tried to find the ball in the wound but it had gone too far. When asked if the wound could have been made by a gun discharging accidentally, he said that in his opinion, it was impossible to have caused it from its position on the table. He was asked where the woman was sitting, and he told them that she was lying on the sofa, her head level with the table. Mr Holmes had undertaken a post-mortem on the body that morning, where he found the bullet had gone through the skull cap and into the brain. He produced the bullet in court and also reiterated that the wound could not have been inflicted in the manner suggested by the prisoner.

PC Cuthbertson told the court that when he was at the police station, Dearden had said that his wife had spent £70 of his money in the last five weeks. David Slingsby, a gunsmith of Lowerhead Row, Leeds, stated that the hammer

Hull Docks as it looks today.

of the revolver would have had to come into contact with the pin of the cartridge before it could explode, and therefore could not have gone off accidentally. The prisoner was further remanded until Thursday 18 July. Dearden was once more brought into court the following week, where another gunsmith, Joseph Wilks, was called and corroborated the evidence of his colleague. However, he emphasised that all guns were dangerous and should not be carried around carelessly. Alfred Carter, the son of the landlord of the Albion Inn, told the court that he had known the prisoner for six months. A few months previously, in June, Dearden had asked his father to look after the gun for him, as he was in lodgings and didn't want to lose it. He told his father that he had bought it at Hull and had it whilst he was a captain, due to having to go through some dangerous places on the docks at night. Carter said that the prisoner had left the gun and six cartridges, which had been handed back to him on 28 June. He had heard him say that his wife was a 'bad woman who went with other men'. Carter saw the prisoner on the Tuesday before the occurrence, when Dearden told him that Minnie had gone off again and he was not going to bother with her anymore, as he could not get her to stay. Mr Malcolm asked the witness if he had seemed angry with his wife when he said this, and Carter replied that Dearden just seemed very sad. The judge summed up the evidence for the jury, who found Dearden guilty. He was committed to take his trial at the next Assizes.

On Wednesday 7 August, Dearden appeared before Mr Baron Cleasby at Leeds Assizes. Mr Wheelhouse and Mr Thompson were for the prosecution and Mr Waddy and Mr Tennant for the defence. Mr Foxcroft gave his statement, adding that the prisoner had continued to demonstrate great remorse for his actions. He had shown the deceased woman nothing but kindness and he would often do all the work before she got up in the morning. But in the five weeks she had lived in the property, she had left him several times to go out drinking with other men.

Mr Wheelhouse told the jury that they had to make the simple decision about whether the gun had been fired deliberately or by accident. No witnesses were brought in by the defence, and Mr Waddy gave a powerful argument as to the innocence of Dearden, who had sobbed repeatedly throughout the trial. Mr Waddy simply stated that anyone who read or heard about the case would instantly see that his client was not guilty of the crime. The prisoner's misfortune had been that his wife was utterly unworthy of him: 'She was a woman who drank and stole his money, and abandoned his bed and board.'

A typical court scene.

The court applauded his speech. The learned judge, in summing up for the jury, questioned why the prisoner had a loaded gun in his pocket – something which had not been satisfactorily explained. He said that despite the evidence of the doctors and gunsmiths, he did not consider it impossible that she had been shot from the table. Nevertheless, he told the jury that they must make up their own minds and deliver the correct verdict.

The jury returned back to the court and the foreman was asked for the verdict. He stated 'Not guilty,' and the court erupted with cheering, which continued for a full ten minutes until order was once more restored.

In this case, it is clear that Dearden faced a lot of provocation by his wife's wanton behaviour, but the judge was right to highlight the fact that no full explanation had been given for why Dearden had the gun in his pocket that night. There was no evidence as to whether he had asked Carter to return the gun to him a month before the shooting – information that would surely have been of great importance to the jury. Nevertheless, we do see that he loved his wife, and the distress shown throughout the trial indicates his sorrow and anguish.

SOLVED

Murder at Oulton Hall

The Execution of John Darcy, 1879

Suspect:	John Darcy
Age:	26
Charge:	Murder
Sentence:	Execution

Many murders are planned in advance and carried out with meticulous attention to details – recognised as 'malice aforethought'. Yet little thought seems to have gone into the planning of the next case, which appears to feature one of the most incompetent criminals I have ever read about. Not only was the perpetrator seen by several witnesses on the road leading to the murder scene and away from it, but he was seen actually committing the murder itself. How he hoped to get away with it is a complete mystery.

The Mansion at Oulton Park was owned in 1879 by a Mr Calverley. He had employed a gate keeper, William Metcalfe, who lived in a lodge on the estate for over forty years. Metcalfe was an elderly man, aged 85, who lived on his own, although a niece, Sarah, came to the lodge most days and did some cleaning and shopping for him. On Saturday 1 March, she had gone to visit her uncle and he gave her a sovereign to change for him. Later that evening she took him the change, giving him half a sovereign and 10s in silver. He put the money into a purse, which he then placed into the top drawer of a chest. A few days before, on 28 February, Sarah had been at her uncle's house when there was a knock on the door. When she had opened it, a man asked her, 'How is your time going on?' and pointed to the clock. She told him it was fine and closed the door in his face.

When she asked her uncle who the man was, he told her it was John Darcy, who came to repair and clean the clocks for him periodically.

John Darcy lived at Mulberry Street, Hunslet, in the lodging house of a woman named Smith. He was 26 years of age and earned a living from mending and cleaning clocks, but he had led a dissolute life. He travelled around the area calling on householders and asking if they wanted any clocks cleaned or repaired. Two weeks previously, Darcy had called at the cottage of a woman named Emma Wright, a widow who lived at Oulton. She had a clock that wanted fixing and as he repaired it in her kitchen, he talked to her about the old man who lived opposite. He asked her if Metcalfe lived alone and she replied in the affirmative.

On the afternoon of 4 March 1879, Darcy was seen leaving Hunslet around 1.30 p.m. by a man named Edward Ellis, who had walked part of the way with him. When the men parted, Ellis saw Darcy walking down the road which led to Oulton, and he noted that he was wearing a brown coat and a billycock hat. Darcy was next seen around 4 p.m. at the John O'Groats public house, where he drank two pints of beer. The landlady noted that he left after only half an hour and also that it was raining outside. He was next seen at Oulton at around 5 p.m., where he once again knocked at the cottage of Emma Wright and enquired about the timepiece he had cleaned a fortnight previously.

The next sighting of Darcy was actually inside the lodge by two girls delivering milk. Carrie Ingham was 13 years of age, and had walked down to the lodge from the hall with her friend Amy Jowitt, aged 12. At approximately 5.30 p.m. they knocked on the lodge door, which was answered by a man who Ingham said she had seen before. He told her to put the milk just inside the door. Later, both girls identified Darcy as being the man who answered the door. Some time afterwards, at around 5.40 p.m., Amy Jowitt spotted him again from her house, which was adjacent to the lodge. Later, three other young boys also gave evidence of seeing Darcy in the vicinity of the lodge on the evening of the murder.

The next person to see him was Sarah Jeffreys, who was passing the lodge gates at 5.50 p.m. when she heard a frightful scream coming from the house. She crossed over the road and went towards the lodge, where she heard Metcalfe saying, 'Oh please don't murder me!' As she approached the partly-open door, it began to close slowly. She listened with her ear to the door and heard the sound of scuffling from within. Suddenly, realising the danger that she was in, she ran to the house of a man named Alfred Morley and told him what she had seen and heard. Along with another man, John Walker, the three of them returned back to the lodge.

Jeffreys remained at the gates whilst the two men looked through a window at the back of the house. There they saw a man holding the room door closed with one hand; in the other he carried a pistol which he had pointed towards the door, as if he was going to fire. They could not see Metcalfe – who by this time was already dead – on the floor of the lodge. Morley and Walker then went to the back door and, peering through the small window, spotted a man opening the drawers and looking inside. Morley described him as being a young man dressed in a brown coat and a billycock hat. Walker went towards the front door, and as he was trying the handle to establish whether the door was locked or not, the handle began to turn in his hand from someone on the inside. Through the door, which was half glazed in glass, both men then saw Darcy holding the pistol in full view.

Aware of the danger they were in, the men backed away and Morley ran to fetch a constable. By this time, the head gardener of Oulton Hall had heard from Sarah Jeffreys of the man in the lodge and the scuffling noises she had heard. He grabbed a gun and he went to the lodge, where he found Mr Metcalfe motionless on the floor. He was covered with blood, pouring from a wound on his head. He looked at the clock owned by the deceased man and noted that it was 6.10 p.m. Shortly afterwards, a search of the area was made by the constable and Morley showed him several footprints, which were later identified as being Darcy's. Also, the old man's empty purse was found about 110 yards away from the lodge.

At about 7 p.m. Darcy was spotted at a public house, the Old Mason's Arms, having two pennyworth of whiskey. The landlord, William Chadwick, later told the court that his pub was approximately 400 yards away from the lodge, and that Darcy drank the whisky quickly and left. He, along with the other witnesses, spoke about Darcy being dressed in a brown coat and a hat.

James Chapman was the next to see Darcy on the road from Oulton to Leeds, where he was driving his horse and cart along the road. As he passed Darcy he shouted, 'Goodnight Sir.' Darcy stopped and asked the man where he knew him from, and Chapman said he recognised him from the chapel that he frequented, on Accommodation Road in Hunslet.

Darcy had started to walk towards Leeds, but now, finally becoming aware of the several witnesses who would be able to place him at the murder scene, told Chapman that he was going to Woodlesford station to catch a train back to Hunslet. Bidding him goodbye, Chapman rode away. Darcy passed the station at Woodlesford, but, presumably still trying to create a diversion, kept walking a further 3 miles to the station at Methley, where he bought a ticket for Hunslet.

Meanwhile, in a twist of fate, Darcy had been recognised by the many witnesses, and a constable, PC Ross, boarded the train at Woodlesford in order to arrest him at Hunslet. He was undoubtedly seen by Darcy, who didn't get off at Hunslet but stayed hiding on the train until he arrived at Leeds. In an attempt to belatedly create an alibi, he then went to a pre-arranged meeting at South Parade Baptist Chapel, arriving twenty minutes late for the service at 8.20 p.m. Despite all his attempts to escape justice, Darcy was arrested by Sergeant Lamb and two officers from the police force at Hunslet, who had been watching Mrs Smith's lodging house. He was searched and a silver watch belonging to Metcalfe, as well as a sampler, which Sarah Metcalfe identified as the one she had embroidered for her uncle, were found in his possession. It was her uncle's habit to wrap the silver watch in this sampler. Darcy also had a sum of money in his possession, yet it was known that when he left Hunslet he had little, if any, money at all.

Darcy claimed that he had not been to Oulton but had spent the day in Methley. However, the many witnesses disproved this story and he was arrested. Whilst Darcy was in custody, there was some confusion about what sort of hat he had been wearing at the time of the murder. Some witnesses stated that it was a billycock hat, whilst others said it was a silk hat. When one of the witnesses who came to identify him asked if Darcy could wear the hat for them, the prisoner stated, 'Why ask me to put on my hat? You might as well tell me to stand with the poker in my hand.' Despite the fact that Darcy had been already charged with murder, no one had mentioned that the old man had been killed with a poker at this point.

By the time Darcy appeared before Mr Justice Manisty at the York Assizes, held on Tuesday 6 May, he had grown a beard. Maybe he thought this would make it harder for witnesses to identify him. Mr Wheelhouse, Mr Lockwood and Mr Green were for the prosecution, while Mr Vernon Blackburn and Mr Lawrence Gane defended the prisoner. It was reported that Darcy entered the court with an 'easy, jaunty air', and when asked if he was guilty or not guilty, he replied confidently, 'I am innocent, praise the Lord.'

Several witnesses gave their account of seeing Darcy at the lodge, and on his journey there and back. The surgeon, John Whitely, told the court that when he completed the post-mortem on Metcalfe, he found several marks of violence on the body. But it had been the two severe lacerations on the left side of the head, both of which had penetrated through the skull, that had finally killed him. He told the court that three portions of bone had penetrated deep

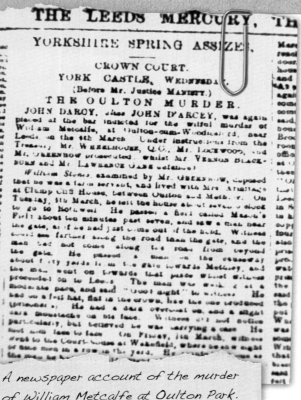

THE LEEDS MERCURY, TH

YORKSHIRE SPRING ASSIZE.

CROWN COURT.
YORK CASTLE, WEDNESDAY.
(Before Mr. Justice MANISTY.)

THE OULTON MURDER.

JOHN DARCY, alias JOHN D'ARCEY, was again placed at the bar indicted for the wilful murder of William Metcalfe, at Oulton-cum-Woodhall rd., near Leeds, on the 4th March. Under instructions from the Treasury, Mr. WHEELHOUSE, Q.C., Mr. LOCKWOOD, and Mr. GREENHOW prosecuted, whilst Mr. VERNON BLACKBURN and Mr. LAWRANCE GANE defended.

William Stones, examined by Mr. GREENHOW, deposed that he was a farm servant, and lived with Mrs. Armitage at Clump Cld House, between Oulton and Methley. On Tuesday, 4th March, he left the house about seven o'clock to go to Methley. He passed a field called Maud's Field about ten minutes past seven, and saw a man near the gate, as if he had just come out of the field. Witness could see farther along the road than the gate, and the man had not come along the road from beyond the gate. He passed a man on the causeway about fifty yards in the ... this towards Methley, and the man went on towards that place whilst witness proceeded on to Leeds. The man was walking at a moderate pace, and said "Good night" to witness. He had on a felt hat, flat in the crown, like the one mentioned (prisoner's). He had a dark overcoat on, and a slight dark moustache on his face. Witness did not notice particularly, but believed he was carrying a case. He had seen the man again on Friday, 4th March, without difficulty at the Court-house at Wakefield, where he saw a number of other men in a row in the yard. ...

A newspaper account of the murder of William Metcalfe at Oulton Park.

into the brain tissue, which had been caused by a heavy object. He was shown the poker, which was bent and misshapen, and he stated that it could have been the weapon which caused the injuries.

By the time several witnesses had been heard, it was growing late and the judge ordered that the case be adjourned until the following day. He told the jury that suitable accommodation had been found for them to spend the night within York Castle.

I wonder how many jurors slept well that night within the castle's ancient, sinister walls. At the same time, the prisoner contemplated his fate whilst walking in the exercise yard of York Prison.

PC John Ross stated that when he heard about the murder, he went to Oulton Hall lodge to see the deceased man. Sergeant Lamb gave evidence that on finding that the prisoner was not at home at his lodgings, he and PC Ross went to some abandoned buildings across the road, where they could clearly see the door. When Darcy was seen to go into the house at around 10.10 p.m., Sergeant Lamb knocked on the door and, without waiting for a response, walked straight into the house. The prisoner was identified by PC Ross, and Sergeant Lamb took Darcy into the sitting room of the house, where he arrested him. A silk hat had been found in the kitchen of the lodging house, which Darcy identified as his own as he went to put it on. Ross told him that this was not the hat he had been wearing at Oulton and, searching his room, found a billycock hat. Darcy refused to wear it, as he said it was too small.

Margaret Smith, the lodging housekeeper, revealed that whilst the police were in the house, Darcy appeared normal and didn't exhibit any excitement or anxiety. Another constable, PC John Oulton, stated that on the morning following the murder, he had found the misshapen poker lying on the road

Murder at Oulton Hall

The exercise yard at York Castle.

from Oulton Hall to Methley. He had found spots of blood and grey hair on it. He had also examined the footprints left near the lodge and compared them with Darcy's boots, to find they corresponded exactly. He told the judge that he visited Darcy in his cell at Leeds Town Hall, and had asked him to take part in an identity parade. Identity parades were often held in corridors, where prisoners would be lined up. When one of the witnesses asked to see Darcy in the billycock hat, and a warden put it on his head, the prisoner dashed it to the ground, denying that the hat was his. Contrary to his previously reported passive demeanour, he appeared to be very violent whilst this exchange took place.

Mr Lawrence Gane ably defended his client, stating that when Darcy approached the two men at the back door, it was not a pistol in his hand, but the poker. He also alluded to the fact that Darcy's boots were of 'a very ordinary make', and could have been bought anywhere. Gane questioned the testimony of the children, claiming that they could have easily been mistaken. He pointed out that the meeting at the Baptist Chapel had been prearranged and that Darcy had gone in his capacity as a Sunday School teacher. The defence declared that, although it had already been established that the old man was covered in blood, no blood had actually been found on the prisoner's clothing. By the time Mr Gane had concluded his speech, the second day of the trial was coming to a close. The witnesses for the defence would be heard the following day and the jury was requested to spend yet another night in York Castle.

The court convened at 10 a.m. on the third day. More witnesses were brought forward to give evidence that Darcy was seen in other places, and therefore could not have been in Oulton at the time of the murder. Mr Gane said, 'A man could not kill another and then join in prayer at a chapel immediately afterwards.' Mr Wheelhouse, for the prosecution, stated that there had been no discrepancies about the testimony of the many witnesses, who had seen him at Oulton, apart from the question of which hat he had been wearing. He also questioned, 'Why would an innocent man grow a beard, other than to disguise himself from witnesses?' He claimed that the prisoner's remark about the poker was made after he had found out that the murder weapon was in fact such an instrument, from one of the police officers.

The judge summed up for the jury, reminding them that they were 'called upon to perform their most solemn duty, which could devolve upon any human being'. The jury retired at 5.20 p.m. and returned at 6.10 p.m. The verdict was that Darcy was guilty of murder. When asked if he had anything to say as to why the sentence of death should not be carried out, the prisoner hesitated. The judge, assuming that he had nothing to say, placed the black cap on his head, but before he could deliver the death sentence, the prisoner spoke:

My Lord and gentlemen of the jury, I am innocent, praise the Lord. At the same time I cannot but return thanks to my Lord and the jury for the carefulness in the examination of this case. No doubt it has been fearfully and wonderfully got Up… The guilty one might be found out one day as he will be surely, but it will be when it is too late. I also wish to make another remark before I cease. The police and various others know that their statements are false and unfounded… I am so horrified at the scene which is laid before you, that I cannot express myself with propriety. I am astonished and I may as well say that I am cast down. But God will raise me up.

He then requested that the judge continue to pass sentence. The judge told him that he agreed with the jury, 'who had come to the same conclusion' as he had. He continued, 'I hoped that you will not leave this world without revealing the truth of the case, and I warn you not to hold out any expectation of mercy.' He then passed the death sentence and Darcy walked swiftly from the dock with his hands clasped in front of him.

It was agreed that Darcy's execution would take place on Tuesday, 27 May 1879 at Armley Gaol, Leeds. Whilst in prison, he appeared to be resigned to his fate and willingly sought solace in prayer. On 22 May, it was reported that despite being a Protestant, Darcy had converted to Catholicism whilst in prison and was receiving daily support from a Roman Catholic minister, Reverend M.C. Fryer. His defence team sent a petition to the Home Secretary, asking for a new trial and stating that he was

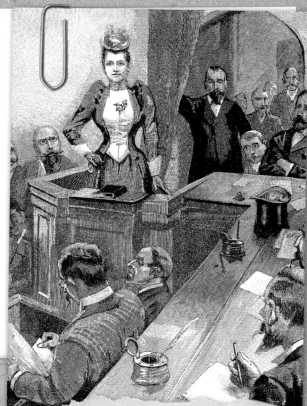

A woman giving evidence in court. (Courtesy of Mysteries of Police and Crime)

A corridor in Leeds Town Hall.

condemned by circumstantial evidence alone. However, it was all to no avail and on the morning of the execution day, Darcy was removed from his cell at precisely 8 a.m. by the hangman, Marwood. On the scaffold, when Reverend Fryer asked him if he had anything to say, Darcy replied, 'I am innocent according to the evidence of the witnesses but I acknowledge the justice of my sentence.' Was he truly an innocent man?

SOLVED

Murder at the Tea Shop

The Death of Margaret Laidler, 1883

Suspect:	Dr Noakes and Mrs Sarah Hobson
Charge:	Wilful Murder
Sentence:	Not Guilty

During the Victorian period, professional men were treated with great respect and reverence, particularly if they were doctors. Witnesses were sometimes openly dismissed by judges if they tried to criticize a professional man's opinion. So when a doctor was involved in a murder case, particularly a sordid case of alleged abortion, it was hard for the judge or jury to take anything he said seriously.

Margaret Laidler (or Nesbitt) was a young woman of 30 years of age, and was employed as the manager of the Globe Tea Company shop at 115 Kirkgate, Wakefield. It was in the flat above the shop where she was found dead on Tuesday, 12 December 1883. A Leeds man, Dr Noakes, was in the habit of visiting Miss Laidler at her dwellings on quite a few occasions. She had been employed at the shop for almost two years, when on 13 November, a shutter fell on her head. As a consequence of this accident, she had been confined to her bedroom for three weeks, where she was treated by Dr Noakes. The 47-year-old doctor, who had his own practice in Halton near Leeds, had been seen on several occasions by Miss Hardisty, who served in the tea shop. On one occasion, he had been accompanied by a female, who she thought was his wife. During Miss Laidler's illness, Miss Hardisty took the post up to the patient's room on a daily basis, and she noted that some letters had the initials S.N. or S.J.N. on the back of them. She was certain that they were from Dr Samuel James Noakes, although she admitted that Miss Laidler received many letters.

The inquest on the body was held at the British Oak Inn, Wakefield, on Monday 18 December, in front of the coroner Major Taylor. The first witness was Miss Hardisty and she told the coroner that a letter with the doctor's initials on had arrived the week before her death, on Monday 4 December. After reading the letter, Miss Laidler told her that she would be going to Leeds that day. In actual fact she did not leave for Leeds until the following afternoon, telling Miss Hardisty that she was expecting to return back to Wakefield on the Friday or Saturday. A Leeds cab driver confirmed that a man and a woman, who he identified as Dr Noakes and Miss Laidler, had taken a cab from the Leeds station to the Mechanics Institute on 5 December. Whilst descending the cab in order to attend to his horse, he witnessed the couple walking up Vernon Road, Leeds.

Dr Noakes and Miss Laidler were next seen entering the house and shop of Mrs Sarah Hobson, a married, second-hand clothes dealer of Vernon Road. Following their arrival, neighbours confirmed that Dr Noakes had visited the shop every day for a week. A further witness at the inquest was the employer of Miss Laidler, Alexander Wallace, the proprietor of the Globe Tea Company. He told the coroner that on 8 December, Dr Noakes had written to him, informing them that Miss Laidler had been taken ill whilst visiting some friends at Ilkley. The doctor stated it was unlikely that she would be able to get back to Wakefield on Saturday as arranged, but she would probably be fit to travel back on Monday 11 December. Mrs Hobson told the coroner that she had been at New Station, Leeds on Saturday 9 December, to see a friend off on the train, when she saw a young lady she did not know who looked very ill indeed. She said her name was Margaret Nesbitt and she'd been travelling from Ilkley, but was not well enough to travel further that night. Mrs Hobson told the inquest that she took the girl home with her and put her to bed, applying hot flannels to her chest and feet. Miss Nesbitt was still ill the following day and Mrs Hobson had written to Dr Noakes, who she was acquainted with, and asked him to come and attend to the girl. He attended the patient every day, where she remained confined to bed. After the weekend, the doctor told Mrs Hobson that Miss Nesbitt insisted that she was going to return to Wakefield on the Monday 'even if she died on the way'. So, on that morning, Dr Noakes arrived and sent for a cab and paid some money to Mrs Hobson for Miss Nesbitt's keep. Hearing all the evidence had taken some hours, so it was at this point that the coroner stated that he was going to adjourn the inquest until Thursday 21 December. It was clear to the coroner and the jury that the evidence given by Mrs Hobson and Dr Noakes did not seem compatible with the evidence from other witnesses. On Wednesday, 20 December, Detective Inspector Burton of the Wakefield Borough Police went to Leeds and arrested Dr Noakes and Mrs Hobson for the wilful murder of Miss Laidler/Nesbitt. Dr Noakes said, 'Morally I am guilty but I think I will be able to prove my innocence.' He then refused to say anything further until he had spoken to his solicitor.

Noakes and Hobson were taken in front of the magistrates on Thursday morning, where they were remanded to give the police more time to investigate the case. Later that day, both appeared before the adjourned inquest. The first witness was Mrs Elizabeth Simpson, who stated that she was employed as a cleaner at Mrs Hobson's shop on Vernon Road, 'for some time past now'. She generally cleaned all the rooms upstairs and down, but from Tuesday 5 December to Monday 11 December, Mrs Hobson had told her that she had a guest staying and she was not to enter a particular bedroom and small sitting room during her stay. Mrs Simpson told the inquest that she had often heard a young woman speaking from inside the room but, as instructed, she had not seen or spoken to the young woman herself. She confirmed seeing Dr Noakes attending the patient several times during her stay. Mrs Simpson then told the jury that, after Mrs Hobson had attended the previous adjourned inquest, held on 13 December, she told her that the young lady who had been staying with her had died. Mrs Hobson instructed Mrs Simpson that if anyone should ask, she was to say that the young lady came on Saturday 9 December. One member of the jury asked if Dr Noakes was present when this conversation took place, but Mrs Simpson said that he wasn't. A Leeds cab driver gave evidence that on 11 December he was in Briggate, Leeds, when Dr Noakes instructed him to be at the shop belonging to Mrs Hobson at 4 p.m. that afternoon. He told the court that when he arrived at the shop, Dr Noakes had led a young woman out of the shop leaning on his arm. The woman, who he later knew to be Miss Laidler, looked pale and extremely ill, and it was obvious that her clothes had been put on over her nightgown. He dropped the couple off at Central Station and had observed a porter assisting Dr Noakes to help the young lady into a carriage.

Leeds railway station as it looks today.

Dr Robert Hollings, a surgeon, gave evidence that he had first seen the deceased at the Globe Tea Company's shop on Tuesday 12 December. Dr Wade, the police surgeon, was also there and it was agreed that they would both jointly undertake the post-mortem. Dr Hollings told the coroner that there was some congestion in the deceased woman's lung and the right oracle of the heart was dilated, although the rest of the heart was healthy. But then he delivered news which stunned the inquest. He stated that both doctors had found the uterus to be very inflamed, which he believed was a condition he had seen before. In previous cases, the irritated state of the uterus had followed the delivery of a child, which in this case he believed to be 'unnatural and brought on with much force'.

At this point in the inquest, Mrs Hobson told the court that she wished to change her statement. She admitted that Miss Nesbitt had gone to her house the previous Tuesday, in the company of Dr Noakes, although she had been expecting her on the Monday. Mrs Hobson said that Dr Noakes had gone to see her a week before Miss Nesbitt came to her house, and asked her if she would have a lodger for a few days. In actual fact, she claimed that Miss Nesbitt had stayed from 5 December to 11 December, and that during that time she didn't go out of the house, except for a few hours during her stay. When asked by the coroner why she had told the previous inquest that the young woman had gone to her house on the Saturday, she replied that Dr Noakes had told her to lie as he was afraid of his wife knowing there was a young lady at her house. Mrs Hobson also told the jury that the doctor had continued to attend every day since the young woman had left, as she herself had not been well.

In another sensational twist to this case, another witness, Mr John Elleker of Bradford, gave evidence that he had been a regular correspondent of Miss Laidler, who he knew as Miss Scott. He had received a telegram on the night of her death and immediately went to Wakefield, where he saw the body at the Globe Tea Company. Miss Hardisty had handed him a bunch of letters that Miss Laidler/Scott had received from him, which he had later destroyed. In reply to the magistrate, he said that he was not in the habit of visiting her very often, but he had visited a few times 'in a friendly way', explaining that he was a happily married man. Dr Noakes then gave evidence and told the inquest he had attended Miss Laidler for many years and, as a result, she had become an intimate friend to him and his wife. He described her as a very delicate girl, saying he had often been over to Wakefield to see her. Dr Noakes then reported that Miss Laidler had also been attended by Dr Stranger of Wakefield, for a cut over her eye which she received when the shutter fell on her head. He had apparently consulted Dr Stranger about the eye injury, and when he received a letter from Miss Laidler stating that Dr Stranger wanted to operate on the eye using chloroform, he had objected to it. Dr Noakes explained that he advised Dr Stranger not to perform the operation, as Miss Laidler had suffered for many years with a weak heart.

Dr Noakes asked a cabman in Briggate to be at Mrs Hobson's house at 4 p.m. on 11 December 1883.

Detective Inspector Henry Burton told the inquest about the first statement he had taken from Dr Noakes. He said that on Saturday 26 November, the doctor claimed to have visited Miss Laidler with his wife, and Miss Laidler had informed them that she was going away for a few days' rest. Dr Noakes advised her that if she wanted to go away, she should seek permission from Dr Stranger before she went. The doctor told Detective Inspector Burton that he had received another letter from Miss Laidler, dated 6 December, stating that she was staying with friends. He was surprised to receive another, dated Friday 8 December, wanting him to meet her at Ilkley as she was very ill. Dr Noakes said he had met her on the station at Ilkley and had commented on her weak appearance. Miss Laidler told him that she had caught a cold and he gave her a 1 gram opium pill, which he carried around with him in his pocket 'as doctors usually do'. He asked her where she was staying, but she refused to tell him and, as there was a train in the station about to leave for Leeds, he left her after only ten or fifteen minutes' conversation, telling her to write and let him know how she was.

In his statement, Dr Noakes had told Inspector Burton that he had received a further letter from her on Sunday 10 December, stating that she was staying at the house of one of his old patients, a Mrs Hobson. Once again, Miss Laidler begged him to attend to her, stating that she was determined to travel back to Wakefield as soon as possible. He went to see her at Mrs Hobson's house at 4 p.m. on Monday, and tried to convince her not to go back to Wakefield that day, but she insisted that he order a cab to take her to the station. In his statement he said that when he heard Miss Laidler was dead, he went over to Wakefield to consult with Dr Stranger, who asked him what he had treated her for in the past. Dr Noakes had told him that she had suffered from pleurisy and hysteria, as well as a weakness of the valvular organs of the heart. Allegedly, Dr Stranger asked him what he thought had caused her death and Dr Noakes replied that it was undoubtedly the heart condition. This was written on the death certificate and both men signed it accordingly.

This evidence concluded the inquest and the coroner summed up for the jury. It took just thirty minutes for them to find both Dr Noakes and Mrs Hobson guilty of wilful murder. The inquest had lasted for over seven hours and it was reported that Dr Noakes looked stunned as he left.

Both Hobson and Noakes appeared before the Bench on Friday 29 December. Before the trial started, the prosecution gave an outline of the case to the magistrates, informing them that the police had stated that Mrs

The platform at Wakefield station as it is today.

Hobson's residence was a 'house of ill-fame'. He claimed that Dr Noakes knew very well that the girl was dying and that Mrs Hobson was insisting that she be removed from her house. He went on to say that the prisoner, Noakes, had made several inconsistent statements, including one that he had treated Miss Laidler at Ilkley, which was untrue, as at the time he had been seen visiting her at Hobson's house. During the inquest, there had been many lies told, including that of a witness called John Elleker, whose actual name was Storr. He had given a false name as he was frightened that his wife might find out that he was involved in the case. It seems that he had admitted to being intimately involved with the girl and confessed that, on at least one occasion, he had spent the night with her at Ilkley. Dr Wade then gave evidence, saying, 'The physical state of the girl could not have been caused by a miscarriage and the facts point irresistibly to the conclusion that an abortion was caused by unnatural means, or such that might have been exercised by the deceased herself.' That concluded the case for the prosecution and the court was adjourned for a week, when they would hear the defence. Dr Noakes stated that he intended to call several medical witnesses.

The following week, Noakes read out a statement that he claimed he would have given to the coroner if he hadn't been arrested before he was able to do so. Dr Noakes admitted telling several untruths, because he was trying to screen the character of the deceased woman. He said that she had asked him to write a false statement about where she had been staying and where he had visited her. He admitted to not having the moral courage to tell the police the truth. Dr Noakes said in his statement that he first became acquainted with Miss Laidler when she was living at a Mrs Taylor's house at Crossgate, Leeds, where he attended her professionally. She became intimate with his family and often visited his house. He had occasionally visited her at the Globe Tea Company shop in Wakefield, and it was on one of these visits that she told him about her condition. Miss Laidler

Murder at the
Tea Shop

contacted him at the end of November, asking if he could find rooms for her in Leeds in order that 'it might not be known in Wakefield'. When he met her off the train on Tuesday 5 December, he wanted to take her to Mrs Taylor's, where he knew she would be cared for, but she begged him not to 'for her character's sake'. So he took her to Mrs Hobson's house, where he ordered that she keep quiet and warm. He visited her on Wednesday, Thursday and Friday, and during this stay she had suffered a natural miscarriage. Miss Laidler told him that she wanted to go home on the Sunday, but he told her 'decidedly not'. She appeared to be very exited and insistent, but he agreed to meet her on the Monday, in order to keep her in Leeds another day. He insisted that his relationship with the girl was honourable and he had done nothing towards any abortion. He stated:

> The symptoms of the case seem to be natural and the construction on the case by Mr Wade who made the post-mortem examination was not justified. I have yielded to the deceased's entreaties to screen her character in order for her to keep her situation, but I am not guilty of the charge made against me.

He then produced several witnesses who stated that the symptoms described by the prosecution were not incompatible with a natural miscarriage, and there were no indications of force being used. The prosecution disagreed, stating that if the medical gentlemen had been at the post-mortem, they would have seen clear signs that the abortion had been brought on by artificial means. The two prisoners were then sent to the Assizes to take their trial. Dr Noakes was further charged with having made a false entry on the certificate of death.

Noakes and Hobson appeared at the Leeds Assizes on Tuesday, 6 February 1883, in front of Mr Justice Day, where Mr Fenwick and Mr Gane appeared for Dr Noakes and Mr Tindal Atkinson appeared for Mrs Hobson. As a medical man, the doctor would not have enjoyed his stay in the cells during the Assizes, as hygiene was incredibly basic.

The prosecution, Mr Barker, opened the case and told the jury that anyone who unlawfully administered or used an instrument in a case of abortion was guilty of murder. He pointed out that judging by the letters written by Dr Noakes, he was a man of little intelligence, but presumably he had sufficient medical experience to commit such an offence. He stated, 'There is little evidence that there was any immoral connection between the doctor and the deceased, but there is little doubt that he was very intimate with her.'

Laidler would have communicated her condition to him and on 5 December she travelled to Leeds, where he met her and took her to the 'house of ill-fame' on Vernon Road, owned by Mrs Hobson. Miss Laidler returned back to Wakefield on 11 December, and Dr Noakes accompanied her to the station and managed to get her onto the train. When she arrived in Wakefield, she was met by a friend, a Mrs Dixon, who Dr Noakes had asked to meet the train. Miss Laidler told her, 'Jenny I have come home to die.' The surgeon, Dr Stranger, was called to attend her, but within ten minutes of his arrival she had died. The prosecution, Mr Barker, told the jury that Noakes and Hobson were anxious to get her out of the house and that they packed off 'a woman who Noakes must have known was dying'. On her death, Stranger sent for Noakes and the two men discussed the reasons for Miss Laidler's death. Noakes managed to convince Stranger that she had died of a long-standing heart disease, and he wrote on the death certificate that she had 'died of valvular disease of the heart'. When a post-mortem was held, it was obvious that she had died from the effects of an abortion. In the words of the prosecution:

> If everything had been above board, once Dr Noakes removed Laidler from Mrs Hudson's house, he would have no need to communicate with Mrs Hudson again, but instead he went to see her several times between the 11th and 15th December. That was not because Hobson was ill, but rather so they could ensure that they both told the same pack of lies.

When Noakes realised that a post-mortem would be held, the pair concocted a story that Mrs Hobson had found her very ill at the station on 9 December, and that, out of the goodness of her heart, she had taken the girl to her own house.

Mrs Jane Dixon, a married woman who had known the deceased, since she herself had a similar tea shop in Wakefield, testified to receiving a letter from Dr Noakes asking her to meet the train with a cab for Miss Laidler, who was ill. She reported that when she arrived off the train Miss Laidler was indeed helpless but conscious.

The groom to Dr Noakes, named William Shaw, gave evidence that he had taken his master to the house on Vernon Road on several occasions between 5 and 11 December. Alexander Wallace, the proprietor of the tea shop, told the jury that Dr Noakes had made arrangements for the funeral of the deceased, and had told him that Miss Laidler's illness had been greatly aggravated by the cold weather. PC Richard McGrath gave evidence as to the nature of Mrs Hobson's house, although he admitted there were no convictions against her. The inquest coroner, Mr Thomas Taylor, spoke about the first statement that he had taken from Mrs Hobson and he told the judge that he thought she was intoxicated and 'not in a fit state to be examined'. The judge asked him incredulously, 'What? And despite this you still took her evidence?' He replied that she was not exactly drunk, just 'in a very excitable state'. The judge asked him, 'Did she seem to understand what she was saying?' and the coroner replied that she did, although he admitted that she had been unable to sign the statement.

Dr Stranger then took the stand and Mr Gane asked him about the shutter which had fallen on Miss Laidler. He asked, 'Was it a severe injury?' and Dr Stranger replied that it was. He was then asked if it was sufficient to cause a miscarriage, and Dr Stranger said that it was possible. William Swift Wade, the police surgeon, told the court that he had held the post-mortem on 13 December and found the organs tolerably healthy in appearance. The body was well nourished, but the right auricle of the heart was diseased. He gave his opinion, once again, that the cause of death had been an abortion, which 'was probably artificial'. The judge asked him if he had formed an opinion as to when the abortion had taken place, and was informed that four or five days before the post-mortem was probable. He also admitted, under questions from Mr Gane, that there were symptoms in the condition of the body that were 'common to natural miscarriages as well as artificial'.

Noakes' statement was read out, in which it was repeated that he had told untruths whilst trying to defend the deceased woman's honour, and that he 'deeply regretted' his conduct. He told the judge that she had been ill when she arrived in Leeds, and when he urged her to go to Mrs Taylor's, she replied, 'No, for my character's sake, do take me somewhere else.' She told him her symptoms and he began treating her and visiting her daily. On the Friday she complained of having a great deal of pain in the night, but expressed a determination to go home the following day. He told her he could not allow that, and she persuaded him to write a letter to her employer, saying that she was at Ilkley. On the Sunday he found her 'excited' and insisting upon returning home. Noakes said he was unable to dissuade her and then stated, 'I am not guilty of doing anything to bring on an abortion and the construction put on the case by Dr Wade is simply not justified.'

The following day the case for the defence was heard. Mr Gane brought in medical evidence that the deceased's symptoms were not only compatible with but actually frequently found in cases of miscarriage. A passenger at Leeds station, who saw Dr Noakes and the woman alighting from a cab, heard him insist that she ought to go back, to which she shook her head from side to side. Four surgeons followed in rapid succession, all stating that the deceased's symptoms indicated a spontaneous abortion. Four more witnesses, who had known Dr Noakes for several years, affirmed his respectability and good character. Mr Atkinson, acting on behalf of Mrs Hobson, commented that unless the jury found the doctor guilty, then Mrs Hobson could not be charged with anything except 'aiding and abetting'. Mr Gane said that Miss Laidler knew very well that she was suffering from the effects of a miscarriage, and that she had gone to Leeds because she was known in Wakefield. Why else would she lie and tell people that she was going to Ilkley – the story she maintained almost to her dying breath?

The judge summed up the evidence, stating that if the jury found that Dr Noakes and Mrs Hobson had conspired to bring on an abortion, then they must be found guilty. But if the jury felt that Mrs Hobson was unaware of what had happened, then they must find her not guilty. At 4.10 p.m. the jury rose to consider their verdict and returned an hour and a half later. The two prisoners, who had been seated for most of the trial, stood up and Dr Noakes clung to the rail in front of the dock as they faced the magistrate. The judge asked the foreman for the verdict on Dr Noakes and he said, 'Not guilty.' The same verdict was given for Mrs Hobson, who began to sob and was led away by a female wardress. It was noted that Dr Noakes' lips moved as if in silent prayer. Applause broke out and the doctor was smiling as he joyfully left the court.

The evidence in this case is very unclear from the start. Certainly the doctor's character had been dissembled throughout the trial, when it was proved that he had lied on several occasions. Mrs Hobson also lied and it was never made clear how a so-called 'respectable' doctor made the acquaintance of a brothel keeper – to such an extent that he was able to procure lodgings for a patient at short notice. Four doctors gave their opinion that a miscarriage had been spontaneous, but they made this judgment on hearing the evidence alone. The doctor who had undertaken the post-mortem, and therefore witnessed the issue at first hand, surely should have been given more credence than he was. These are several very puzzling issues in this case, which indicate that perhaps the law wanted to remove the blame from a member of an honourable profession.

Case Twelve

A Lethal Attack

The Case of Samuel Harrison, 1890

Suspect:	*Samuel Harrison*
Charge:	*Wilful Murder*
Verdict:	*Guilty*
Sentence:	*Committed to Broadmoor Lunatic Asylum*

Many Jewish people were attracted to Leeds because of the rapidly expanding clothing and shoemaking industries, and the fact that conditions in these sweatshops were better and wages were higher than in other towns such as Manchester or London. Nevertheless, the Jewish immigrants faced prejudice from many people in Leeds, and from the nation as a whole. Leeds was a city of opposites; as the burgeoning industrial revolution saw an influx of wealthy entrepreneurs who would stay in the luxurious hotels of the city making lucrative business deals, the immigrants had to make do with the poorest, most overcrowded housing and basic sanitary conditions. In a report on immigration undertaken in 1888, it was reported, 'Over the previous twenty years, there has been a steady influx of Polish and Russian Jews, whose only word of English was "Leeds".' The distrust of the Jews is shown in the following case, when neighbours of a dying Jewish woman refused to let her into their house.

On Saturday, 9 May 1890, the Jewish community in Leeds heard of a diabolical murder by a Russian Jew of his wife and child. The name of the man, which was probably anglicised, was Samuel Harrison, aged 30. He had lived for some time at Back Nile Street, Leeds, with his wife Dora and his 2-year-old son David. The couple did not live in harmony together, as a year previously

The Hotel Metropole still operates in Leeds today.

he had been sent to gaol for a month for attacking a young boy. It was reported that this boy was one of a crowd that gathered around his house whilst he was assaulting his wife. When he had been sent down for this crime, he told the magistrate, 'You better keep me in prison or when I come out I will kill her.' Neighbours reported that when he came back to Leeds, there were frequent quarrels. On Friday 8 May, he attacked his wife and child with a shoemaker's knife (he was a shoemaker by occupation) at about 6.30 p.m. The woman's screams attracted the attention of the neighbours and also of PC Pimblott, who was on duty nearby. He rushed over to the house and ran up the stairs but found the bedroom door locked. Putting his shoulder against it, he managed to get the door open and found Mrs Harrison in a corner, holding her little child; both were covered in blood. No doubt in an attempt to hide his crime, Harrison had lit fires at either side of the bed and the room was full of smoke. The constable put some handcuffs on Harrison and handed him over to a civilian, instructing him to hold him until help came. Another neighbour took the child to the dispensary, whilst Pimblott carried the poor woman out into the street and away from the smoke-filled bedroom. Neighbours refused to have the woman in their house, so she lay in the street bleeding while Pimblott blew on his whistle for assistance. A surgeon, Mr Musgrove, approached urgently after hearing it. With great difficulty, because of the large crowd, he managed to make his way to the poor woman's side, where he found her bleeding profusely.

A Lethal Attack

By now, the two fires had been put out in the bedroom and, with the assistance of another police constable, the surgeon managed to get Mrs Harrison back into her bedroom. Using just rags and any clothes he could find, the surgeon bound up her wounds. On her neck, breast and shoulders there were six long gashes and numberless smaller cuts. The furniture in the bedroom had been smashed to pieces and the floor was saturated with blood. By this time, an ambulance had arrived from the infirmary and the injured woman was taken there in haste. Harrison was now marched off to Millgarth Street police station. A reporter described Harrison as:

… an insignificant looking little man, with a pale face, a restless pair of eyes, a reddish-brown beard and he has little of the Jewish characteristics in his appearance. When arrested he was wearing a close fitting cap, a loose coat and check trousers, which in places were soaked with blood. He showed little concern for the crime.

The child was treated for his wounds by Mr Smeeton, but it was reported that little hope could be held out for his survival. The child's mother was in a dying state and it was arranged that she would have a deposition taken from her. Accordingly, Mr John Thornton, the magistrate's clerk, and Alderman Sir Edwin Gaunt, who was the nearest magistrate, were sent for and they proceeded to the infirmary. They arrived to find Superintendent McWilliams and Detective Officer Slingsby there with the prisoner, who was still in handcuffs. Harrison appeared unconcerned about the condition of his wife and child. Mrs Harrison was unable to speak any English, so another woman, Mrs Schalk, acted as interpreter and told the following harrowing tale:

I am suffering from some wounds which my own husband inflicted on me. He did them with a knife and I was in my own house when he did it. No one else was there and it was today, but I can't say when. I do not know why he did it, and I do not know how it began. I had not done anything to him. He did it with the knife that he works with. He carries that knife about with him. It is a shoemaker's knife. He struck me with the knife twice, but I had no quarrel with him. He is a man that is mad, but I don't know what makes him mad. I had my child with me who is 2 years old. He is a madman and I don't know what it was for.

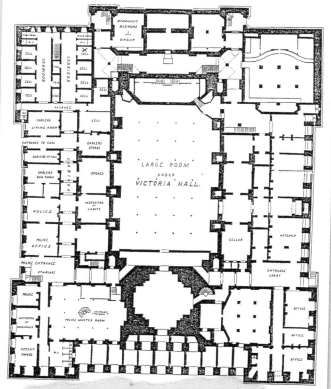

The plan of the cells underneath Leeds Town Hall.

The statement was about to be read back to her for confirmation, when the poor woman fainted and had to have medical help. In the meantime, Harrison was taken away and put into one of the many cells underneath the Town Hall. Mr Thornton and Alderman Gaunt also retired to the Town Hall, instructing the infirmary to notify them if her condition improved, as they needed to get the dying woman's signature. However, a later message from the infirmary stated that both the mother and child were sinking fast. The murder knife was later handed over to PC Lockhart, which was described as being a knife with a short blade of only 3ins long, but sharpened to that of a razor and covered in blood. The ferocity of the attack was indicated by the fact that the tip of the blade was broken, presumably from contact with a rib or a shoulder blade.

Mrs Harrison died at 6 a.m. the following morning. Her son was reported to be in a precarious state but it was thought that there might be hope for his recovery. PC Pimblott, on hearing the news, charged Harrison with wilful murder. When asked if he had anything to say, Harrison stated, 'Yes Sir, I did kill her.' He was taken into court before Mr Bruce (the stipendiary magistrate), Mr John Rhodes, Mr James Walker and Sir Edwin Gaunt. The gallery of the court was crowded with people, many of whom were Jewish, whilst others congregated in the corridors of the Town Hall building. PC Pimblott told the court of the night's events, and stated that he had asked Harrison three times to hand over the murder weapon. On all three occasions Harrison denied having a knife. The knife was eventually found and handed to him by Dr Musgrave.

A Lethal Attack

Harrison said that the attack started because there was a crowd of people in the street who were trying to get into his house. It was unclear why they were trying to enter, although Harrison told them it was a common occurrence.

The magistrate asked Pimblott if there had been a lot of people in the street and he told them that there had been about 2,000 men and women. The prisoner was remanded until the following day. The inquest on the murdered woman was also heard on the same day, where the surgeon of the infirmary told the coroner, Mr J.C. Malcolm, that when Mrs Harrison had been admitted she had over seventeen wounds in her body. The most serious injury had been one on the right side of the chest. The surgeon, Mr Bernard Musgrave, gave his evidence and also commented on the huge crowd around the woman. When he first saw her, he thought that she was dead. To a shocked coroner, he told him that several people had refused to allow the injured woman to be taken into their house. PC Pimblott spoke about breaking down the door of the house and securing the prisoner with handcuffs to the bed whilst the room was on fire. The coroner, after hearing the evidence, agreed to send Pimblott for trial at the Assizes.

On Tuesday, 5 August 1890, Harrison was brought into the Leeds Assizes before Mr Justice Charles, charged with the murder of his wife. Once again the court was crowded, but when asked his plea, Harrison refused to speak and just hung his head. He seemed to ignore what was being said. It was stated that he had been mute for the last fortnight, and His Lordship asked for a medical examination to be carried out to ascertain if he was mute by malice or by 'the visitation of God'.

After examining him, the medical officer said he was shamming, and the judge ordered that a plea of not guilty be put against him. The medical officer of Armley Gaol, Mr John Edwards, stated that the prisoner had been under his care and said that at first he was very communicative, but after a lapse of ten days, he refused to speak or answer any questions. He had examined him that morning and was convinced that Harrison understood what was going on. The defence maintained that he was insane at the time of the incident and witnesses were called to prove that several of his relatives had been inflicted with insanity. Despite this, the jury returned a verdict of guilty. His Lordship then put on the black cap and gave the sentence of death. Harrison was led from the court, seemingly indifferent to the excited crowds around him.

On Friday 14 August, it was reported that Baron de Rothschild was heading a movement to petition the Home Secretary, to allow a further medical examination of Harrison. It seems that since his sentence, he continued to show no emotion and preserved a silence, even when spoke to by his Rabbi. He was sharing the condemned cell with a man named James Harrison, also sentenced to death for beating his wife. On Saturday 16 August, it was announced that the date set for the execution was 26 August, and the hangman would be Billington. On Tuesday 19 August, his solicitors Messrs Dunn and French received the following letter.

Whitehall, 16 August 1890

Gentlemen,

With reference to representation you have submitted regarding Mr Samuel Harrison who was sentenced to death for murder, I am directed by the Secretary of State to acquaint you that after a medical enquiry resulting in the convict being certified to be of unsound mind, he has advised her Majesty to respite the execution of the capital sentence with a view to remove the convict to Broadmoor Criminal Lunatic Asylum.

I am gentlemen your obedient servant,

GODFREY LUSHINGTON

Samuel Harrison was removed to Broadmoor the following day. In this case, there seems to be much evidence that the man was insane, but that doesn't explain the crowds of people who collected around his home and the unwillingness of neighbours to let a dying woman into their house. There was plenty of prejudice in the nineteenth century – Jewish people, Catholics and Irish natives were some of the groups on the receiving end. As the town expanded and became the city we know today, the prejudice finally alleviated and it became known as the City of Sanctuary. On 11 November 2, a movement was launched to celebrate supporting immigrants coming to Leeds to seek safety – a far cry from the city described in these pages.

A Lethal Attack